Are Dragons Real?

Throughout time the people of nearly every culture in the world have believed in dragons. Mythologies, folklore, and legends are full of tales about these splendid creatures and their interactions with mankind.

Since dragons do not live on the physical plane, many people assume they aren't real. But magicians, mystics, and others who are familiar with the astral realm know firsthand that dragons and other astral beings do exist. The ancient wisdom of dragons makes them excellent to call upon when performing any type of divination, such as the laying out of tarot cards.

This unique tarot deck captures the magick and mythology of the Celtic dragon, yet keeps the framework of the traditional tarot. Fantasy artist, Lisa Hunt, has created exquisite, thought-provoking, and, often, amusing images for the tarot aficiandao's enjoyment. Wiccan author, D. J. Conway, has interpreted the cards with profound depth and sensitivity.

The radiant, sinuous energy of the dragon moves through *The Celtic Dragon Tarot* to illuminate the familiar magician's journey in a unique way.

Let the unseen—yet real—power of the dragon enrich your tarot readings, spellwork, meditation practice, and personal growth.

About the Creators

D. J. Conway

A West Coast resident, D. J. Conway is the author of over nineteen books and coauthor of the *Shapeshifter Tarot. The Celtic Dragon Tarot*, created with the talented artist Lisa Hunt, was a labor of love and joy. Ms. Conway has seriously studied many spiritual paths from the New Age religions to Eastern philosophy to Wicca for almost forty years. Most of her time is happily spent researching (history, the magickal arts, philosophy, customs, anything Celtic, mythology, folklore, and fantasy) and of course writing books, a profession she greatly enjoys.

A quiet person, she is not fond of large crowds or speaking in public. Instead, she lives a rather secluded life with her husband and six cats, with occasional visits with her children and grandchildren.

She has several books published by Llewellyn at this time: *Celtic Magic; Dancing With Dragons; By Oak, Ash & Thorn: Modern Celtic Shamanism; Moon Magick; Animal Magick; Magickal, Mythical, Mystical Beasts; The Mysterious Magickal Cat; Shapeshifter Tarot;* and the Dream Warrior fantasy fiction trilogy, among others.

Lisa Hunt

Lisa Hunt is a professional illustrator who has illustrated numerous trade paperbacks for Llewellyn Worldwide, including books by D. J. Conway. She is the illustrator of *Shapeshifter Tarot,* author and illustrator of *Celestial Goddesses,* and coauthor and illustrator of the children's book *One is a Mouse* for Simon & Schuster. She also creates fantasy artwork for magazines and trading card games. Lisa earned a B.S. degree in Computer Animation and has worked as a conceptual designer for television movie production.

While painting images for *The Celtic Dragon Tarot*, the artist says, "The images flowed from my paintbrush. It was as if dragons were presiding over the evolving project."

Lisa lives in Florida with her author/illustrator husband, Jonathan, and their cats.

A Guide to the Celtic Dragon Tarot

D. J. Conway

Illustrated by
Lisa Hunt

2002
Llewellyn Publications
St. Paul, Minnesota 55164-0383

FIRST EDITION
Fifth Printing, 2002

Book design by Rebecca Zins and Marilyn Matheny
Cover art by Lisa Hunt
Cover design by Lynne Menturweck

Library of Congress Cataloging-in-Publication Data

Conway, D. J. (Deanna J.)
A guide to the Celtic dragon tarot / D. J. Conway ; illustrated by Lisa Hunt. — 1st ed.
p. cm.
Includes bibliographical references and index.
ISBN 1–56718–184–8. — ISBN 1–56718–182–1 (kit). — ISBN 1–56718–185–6 (tarot deck)
1. Tarot. 2. Mythology, Celtic—Miscellanea. 3. Dragons—Miscellanea. I. Title.
BF1879.T2C615 1999
133.3'2424—dc21 99–40420
CIP

Llewellyn Publications
A Division of Llewellyn Worldwide, Ltd.
P.O. Box 64383, Dept. K184–8
St. Paul, MN 55164–0383, U.S.A
www.llewellyn.com

 Printed in the United States of America

Dedications

D. J. Conway

To Colin, who always looked for dragons when he visited.
To Merren, who sees the dragons in her home. And
to Morrigan, who now has a special dragon of her own.

Lisa Hunt

For Annelies and David Behnke
who gave me wings to fly,
and for Jonathan and D. J.,
who showed me how to use them.

Other Books by D. J. Conway

Nonfiction Books:

Animal Magick
By Oak, Ash & Thorn
Celtic Magic
Dancing with Dragons
Falcon, Feather & Valkyrie Sword
Flying Without a Broom
Lord of Light & Shadow
Magick of the Gods & Goddesses
Magickal, Mythical, Mystical Beasts
Maiden, Mother, Crone
Moon Magick
Mysterious Magickal Cat
Norse Magic
Perfect Love
The Celtic Book of Names (Carol Publishing)

Tarot Decks and Books:

Shapeshifter Tarot
with Lisa Hunt and Sirona Knight

Fantasy Fiction Trilogy:

The Dream Warrior
Soothslayer
Warrior of Shadows

Forthcoming Books:

Crystal Enchantments (The Crossing Press)
Laying on the Stones (The Crossing Press)
A Little Book of Candle Magic and Altars (The Crossing Press)

Contents

Preface

Creation of the Celtic Dragon Tarot

The idea of *The Celtic Dragon Tarot* came into being while I was writing *Dancing With Dragons*, released in 1994. It grabbed my imagination so strongly that I made pages of notes about the cards and accompanying book. However, there was no interest in the idea at that time, so the information went into a file and waited.

After I worked with Lisa Hunt on *Shapeshifter Tarot*, I knew she was the perfect artist with whom I could work on the dragon cards. Hoping that she would accept the project, I submitted it again in the fall of 1997, and this time it was accepted. When I contacted Lisa and, holding my breath, asked if she would be interested in working on *The Celtic Dragon Tarot* with me, she was delighted. I breathed a sigh of relief, knowing then that the project would run smoothly and be a beautiful tarot deck.

Determined that this card deck would be unique, we decided to avoid all New Age looks and designs, striving instead for an atmosphere and symbolism that blended perfectly with dragons—that of the Celts who used so many spiritual symbols. We chose to use only landscapes from the Celtic countries of Ireland, Scotland, and Wales.

It seemed natural that medieval clothing and castles should be part of this Celtic, almost Otherworldly, atmosphere.

I worked up brief descriptions of each card, leaving the minor details in Lisa's capable hands. It proved to be the right thing to do, for the most amazing synergy sprang up between us. It was if we had connected in a subconscious, spiritual way that enabled us both to see each finished card in our minds, and the mental pictures were exactly the same.

An example is the Major Arcana card Death. I knew how I wanted that dragon to look, shedding its dark skin and emerging as white, but I found it difficult to put into words. Lisa never hesitated. She produced the most beautiful painting for Death and captured every mental detail perfectly.

Never once was there any disagreement between us about the art or project in the year plus it took us to complete *The Celtic Dragon Tarot*. Everything flowed perfectly. Even though we were hampered occasionally by the usual winter colds, niggling family problems, and other commitments, the wonderful energy flow between us never diminished in its intensity. It was such an unusual experience that, when I received each painting and checked my written description of the card, there were few if any changes needed in the description and absolutely none needed in the art. This was a partnership synergy that may only come once in a lifetime.

The Celtic Dragon Tarot is a unique deck in that it will speak to anyone, regardless of their interest in Celtic symbols or not. Perhaps that is because of the love and dedication that went into the art and the writing. Whatever the reason for its remarkable birth and creation, I am grateful that we can now offer it to tarot readers, magicians, and dragon lovers everywhere. May it speak to your innermost being, that part of you that is struggling, as the dragon on the Death card does, to make something new out of your life.

— D. J. Conway

I have always had an affinity for dragons. As a child, these fabulous beasts were an integral part of my creative being and often showed up in doodles, even when I was not consciously aware of what I was drawing. The faithful dragon has been a muse and companion throughout my creative growth and its majesty has never ceased to inspire me.

When D. J. Conway first contacted me about her idea to create a tarot deck filled with dragons, I nearly jumped out of my chair in excitement. Having worked with D. J. on *Shapeshifter Tarot* and knowing that we are both partial to dragons, I felt confident that we were about to embark on a special creative journey. I readily agreed to work with her, and from that moment forward, I felt an immense energy that remained with me throughout the evolution of *The Celtic Dragon*.

Upon receiving D. J.'s descriptions for the cards, I spent a month sketching dragons of all shapes and sizes and began to explore different designs showcasing a myriad of these beasts. I visited a local natural history museum and sketched all manner of animals and bones because I wanted to be familiar and comfortable with animal anatomy before embarking on refined drawings. I sketched birds, bats, dinosaur bones, reptiles, and predatory mammals. This stimulated my imagination because there were elements of many of these creatures that I felt could be incorporated into dragon anatomy. Some of my dragon designs were an amalgamation of several different animals.

I also studied Celtic landscapes, symbols, architecture, costume, and historical texts. The Celtic landscape and ancient symbols ubiquitous in the Celtic culture provided a wonderful backdrop for the timeless beast. I intentionally romanticized the environments on the cards because I felt it appropriate to provide a fantastical setting for creatures not discernible on this plane of existence.

The more academic approach soon gave way to pure and loose imagination as I nurtured these drawings and allowed my subconscious to pour onto the page. During the year that I spent working on *The Celtic Dragon*, I lived and slept dragons. Many of my dreams were filled with dragon motifs which I feel helped to facilitate some of the paintings. D. J. was also a constant companion over the course of this project. We were in continual contact, sometimes e-mailing each other two or three times a day. Many of our e-mails were filled with enthusiastic exchanges about the delight of working on a project about dragons.

As the drawings progressed, I sent them to D. J. to get her feedback and to have her check for accuracy and consistency in accordance to the descriptions. From there I proceeded to refine the drawings (sending them to D. J. with each progressing step) and then transferred finished renderings onto watercolor paper.

When I began to paint, much of the spontaneous joy I was feeling manifested itself on paper. These images literally flowed mellifluously from my paintbrush. I felt so connected to the process and the sheer delight of the subject matter, that I almost lived vicariously through the characters in the pieces. I felt an amazing, continuous swell of creative energy, from the first piece to the last. Never did I experience burn out or frustration over the course of producing seventy-eight paintings ... well, except perhaps for the occasional coffee spills, cat scratches, and accidental paint splashes that revealed themselves during those late night hours.

I often felt telepathically connected with D. J. when I was painting, because the images evolved so naturally. It was as if she helped feed the connection between brain and paper. I also believe that the dragons helped to generate this indefatigable quest to paint. They also kept the midnight oil burning into the wee hours of the morning when the muses had me shackled to my desk.

After I completed the paintings, I sent color copies to D. J. so that she could extract details from the images and incorporate them into the descriptions. What resulted truly blew me away! D. J. derived symbolic meaning from the paintings that I did not always consciously include. I felt her interpretation and analysis of my work reflected the thoughts and feelings stored in the deep layers of my subconscious mind. This ability to see through my paintings in a multidimensional manner was a pinnacle of our symbiotic relationship and demonstrated that a project of this magnitude was meant to see light. Such creative synchronicity rarely occurs between two artistic egos.

Since this project was enveloped with positivity and passion for all things dragon, we hope that our dedication and deep connection with the subject matter will be felt and experienced by the card user. We wanted to reveal the universal guidance and value that dragons can provide for an individual whether you are an avid card user, or simply an individual who feels affection for dragons. This deck is for anyone who believes or wants to believe in the power of dragons.

I hope this deck touches you in the same profound way that it touched me when I painted with soulful energy onto the watercolor paper. D. J. and I love dragons and we hope that this deck will inspire you to nurture a relationship with this ancient and universally recognized beast.

— Lisa Hunt

Acknowledgements

D. J. Conway

My thanks to Lisa, the artist who made my mental pictures come alive on paper, and to Charles and Jon, who were always encouraging of our project.

Lisa Hunt

I would like to thank: Jonathan, husband and soul mate; D. J. Conway, dear friend and kindred spirit; Pam Keane, Jessica Welch, and Cassiano Maciel for striking great poses; my fellow artists and friends—Lynette and Robert Carsten, Nancy Bush, the Finneys, Lorna Hernandez, and "soul sister" Kris Waldherr; and everyone who has watched me learn and grow.

Special thanks to my outstanding art director Lynne Menturweck who helped me to maintain balance and creative energy throughout this project. I would also like to thank all of the dragons that helped me burn the midnight oil during those long hours in the studio!

The Magick of Dragons

Throughout history nearly every culture has recorded stories of dragons. Dragons are known in one form or another around the world. Mythologies, folklore, and legends are full of tales about these creatures and their interaction with humans. Unfortunately, the latter parts of European history have not been truthful about or kind to these splendid astral beings.

When I wrote *Dancing With Dragons*, I was not prepared for the positive response from readers worldwide. I was merely trying to set the record straight and show people how wise and wonderful dragons can be. They are some of the best co-magicians any person working spells could ask for. They can be good friends, powerful protectors, and wise teachers, if the practitioner takes the time and effort to make their acquaintance.

But are dragons real? Since these beings do not live on the physical plane, scientists cannot trap and dissect these creatures. Therefore, according to many people dragons are not "real." However, science and scientists have been wrong a good many times.

Practitioners and dragon-lovers feel no need to base their beliefs on so-called scientific "facts." Since they, and psychics in other fields than magick, know how to reach, traverse, and find help and information on the astral planes, they know firsthand that dragons and other unusual creatures do exist.

No one simple description portrays dragons, although there are a few common traits to all in this species: breathing fire and moving through the air. Ancient teachings say dragons can have two or four legs or none at all, a pair of wings or be wingless, breathe fire and smoke, and have scales on their bodies. Dragons are long-lived and very wise. Depending upon the reception they received from humans in the area where they lived, dragons were either beneficial or violent.

Although one can speak of dragons as a separate species of being, there are numerous subspecies and families within the dragon community. The dragon species is divided into numerous families, who live in different sections of the world. These families are further divided into a variety of subspecies, such as: dragons of Mountains, Forests, Seas and Waters, the Elements, Wind, Storm, Weather, Volcanoes, Fire, Chaos, Light, and Deserts. Each type of dragon is attracted by certain colors and stones (see the appendices), thus making them more amenable to helping with magick.

One family of dragons with similar characteristics was found in Europe, particularly in northern Germany, Scandinavia, and the islands of the North Atlantic. These dragons frequently had a thick body and large wings. Some descriptions mention four legs, while others tell of no legs at all. Tradition says that Fafnir, the wily dragon who guarded a treasure and who was killed by the Scandinavian hero Sigurd, was a huge snake-like creature with magical blood.

A second, and slightly different, family lived in France, Italy, and Spain. These dragons were smaller than those in the North. According to folklore, these dragons were rarely larger than a horse and tended to avoid humans.

The third group was composed of regular four-legged dragons, the Wyverns (dragons with two legs), and the Worms (dragons with no legs). They inhabited Ireland and the British Isles. Until the early Middle Ages, there were reports of frequent flights of dragons in Scotland and England. Celtic stories tell of Conchobar and Finn MacCumhaill of Ireland, who both interacted with different types of dragons.

The fourth family inhabited Greece, Asia Minor, southern Russia, and northern Africa; the dragon with many heads was common in these areas. Greek legends tell of both Hercules and Jason destroying a seven-headed hydra, while Perseus defended Andromeda from a huge Sea dragon.

The Americas and Australia were sparsely populated by a fifth group, which was of very limited size and number. Dragons of the Americas, Mexico, and Australia were wingless, but propelled themselves through the skies by balancing on the Earth's magnetic field and the winds. The best known dragon was the Feathered Serpent depicted on Aztec and Mayan temples.

The Oriental dragons make up the sixth family of dragons and lived in China, Asia, and Indonesia. Oriental dragons rarely breathed fire and were, for the most part, more benevolent toward humans than the Western dragons. Although wingless, they propelled themselves easily through the air. They had a long serpentine body, four legs, and a snake-like tail. The Imperial dragons had five claws on each foot, while the lesser dragons had only three or four.

Why would anyone want to contact dragons? Dragons have control of deeper currents of elemental energies than is usually felt by humans. They are always connected in some manner with various forms of the four Elements: Earth, Air, Fire, and Water. Dragons also make very powerful co-magicians.

When speaking of the Elements, I do not mean the physical energies we usually think of. The Elemental powers of Earth, Air, Fire, and Water are streams of certain types of astral and spiritual energy that can be tapped into and used to produce certain results.

Because of the ancient wisdom of dragons, they are also valuable to call upon when performing any type of divination, such as the laying out of tarot cards. Tarot decks and other divination tools seem to fascinate them.

It was with this knowledge in mind that I put forth the idea of *The Celtic Dragon Tarot*. (Celtic is pronounced *kell-tik*, unless you are speaking of a Boston sports team.) If you are only interested in these cards for tarot readings, you can easily use them in just that manner. However, if you want to delve deeper into dragon power, these cards will aid you in following that path as well.

To the ancient mapmakers, every unknown territory was listed as "here be dragons." Both tarot and magick have many uncharted areas. Not only will you find dragons waiting there, but you also will find these unusual creatures can be helpful if you give them the chance.

Chapter 1

Using the Celtic Dragon Tarot

The Celtic Dragon Tarot can be used like any other tarot deck that adheres closely to the traditional methods of portraying the tarot symbols. These seventy-eight cards can be laid out in any divination pattern with which you are familiar, or you can experiment with the layouts given in chapter 5. This deck has the usual number of cards, all in the order commonly known to tarot readers. They are read only in the upright position, not in the reversed position, however. The only differences will be that I associate Wands with the Element of Air, and Swords with the Element of Fire. This association has always made more sense to me than the reverse, since Wands are primarily a mental ritual tool and Swords are an energy or action tool. This is not a new idea, nor mine alone. I have also changed the names on two cards of the Major Arcana—card 5, now The High Priest, and card 15, now Chains. Neither of the usual names applied to these cards have anything to do with pre-Christian Celtic spirituality.

Chapter 2 gives a quick overview of the cards and their meanings, while chapters 3 and 4 provide a more detailed description and meaning of each card.

The Celtic Dragon Tarot deck can also be used as part of magickal spellworking and in meditational exercises. Chapter 6 goes into detail on spellworking and lists many examples. Chapter 7 not only discusses meditation, but also gives actual meditations that you can use for your own spiritual journeys in your quest for knowledge.

Elements Associated with The Celtic Dragon Tarot

Element	Suit
Air	Wands
Fire	Swords
Water	Cups
Earth	Pentacles

Chapter 2

Guide to the Cards

Major Arcana

Card Name	Key Words
0. The Fool	Unexpected change of directions.
1. The Magician	Self-control; learning magick.
2. High Priestess	Unknown future.
3. The Empress	Unexpected blessings; Goddess influence.
4. The Emperor	Power; God influence.
5. High Priest	Facing karmic issues.
6. The Lovers	An emotional decision.
7. The Chariot	Maintaining balanced control.
8. Strength	Courage; inner strength.
9. The Hermit	Solitude.
10. The Wheel	Change of fortune.
11. Justice	Legal matters.
12. The Hanged Man	Suspended activity.
13. Death	Transformation.
14. Temperance	New perspectives.
15. Chains	Oppressive situations.
16. The Tower	Discord; catastrophe.
17. The Star	Spiritual experiences.
18. The Moon	Dreams; intuition.
19. The Sun	Positive events.
20. Judgment	Renewal; karmic issues.
21. The World	Achieving success and goals.

Minor Arcana

Wands (Air)

Card Name	Key Words
Ace of Wands	New beginnings; new cycles.
2 of Wands	Focus will and energy.
3 of Wands	Planning; partnership.
4 of Wands	Happiness; rest; success.
5 of Wands	Obstacles; opposition.
6 of Wands	Success after hard work.
7 of Wands	Difficulties; competition.
8 of Wands	Movement; urgency.
9 of Wands	A pause.
10 of Wands	Struggle; loss.
Page of Wands	Important news; foreign places.
Knight of Wands	Sudden changes.
Queen of Wands	Reaping rewards; social events.
King of Wands	Ambition; leadership.

Swords (Fire)

Card Name	Key Words
Ace of Swords	Decisions; activity.
2 of Swords	Tension; indecision.
3 of Swords	Emotional upheavals.
4 of Swords	Rest; a pause.
5 of Swords	Slander; arguments; failure.
6 of Swords	Journeys; difficult choice.
7 of Swords	Bad feelings; snooping.
8 of Swords	Restriction; fear.
9 of Swords	Great sadness; loss.
10 of Swords	Disruption; dark times.

Page of Swords	Impulsiveness; troubles.
Knight of Swords	Misfortune; persecution.
Queen of Swords	Learning lessons; manipulation.
King of Swords	Opposition; obey the laws.

Cups (Water)

Card Name	Key Words
Ace of Cups	Joy; fertile period.
2 of Cups	Love; friendship; commitment.
3 of Cups	Prosperity; success.
4 of Cups	Old memories; dissatisfaction.
5 of Cups	Negative events.
6 of Cups	Reunions; unexpected gifts.
7 of Cups	Daydreams; responsibility.
8 of Cups	Lack of discipline.
9 of Cups	Wishes granted.
10 of Cups	Goals reached; contentment.
Page of Cups	Message of love.
Knight of Cups	Unexpected pleasant times.
Queen of Cups	Strong psychic feelings.
King of Cups	Emotional events.

Pentacles (Earth)

Card Name	Key Words
Ace of Pentacles	Material success.
2 of Pentacles	Harmony through changes.
3 of Pentacles	Profitable skills; satisfaction.
4 of Pentacles	Grasping at money.
5 of Pentacles	Loss; unpleasant differences.
6 of Pentacles	Just rewards.
7 of Pentacles	Anxiety; progress stopped.

8 of Pentacles	New skills; new opportunities.
9 of Pentacles	Comfortable aloneness.
10 of Pentacles	Property; business.
Page of Pentacles	News of money.
Knight of Pentacles	Gains and losses.
Queen of Pentacles	Future plans.
King of Pentacles	Success in business and money.

Chapter 3

Major Arcana

The Major Arcana cards of the tarot deck symbolize the major steps we take in each cycle of life. The eternal cycle repeats itself until we learn the lessons we have come here to learn, not in just one way, but in numerous ways.

You can determine where you are in a life cycle by finding the Major Arcana card that most closely represents your present position in life. In readings, these cards symbolize the major steps you have taken or will take in the future.

0

The Fool

Unexpected change of directions.

The Fool

The Fool is the Dreamer, the novice who is beginning on the path of a new cycle in life. This person is one who stands at a crossroads in his spiritual growth. Dressed in the white of the innocent seeker, the Fool holds the symbols of his magickal and spiritual studies: the crystal-topped wand and the scrolls of knowledge. The tiny dragons flying before the Fool act as guides as they draw the Fool's attention away from the ordinary and into the realms of the extraordinary, the astral and spiritual, where all magick and change begins and grows before its manifestation onto the physical plane. The Fool has experienced the realization that dragons are not figments of imagination, but powerful astral teachers and co-magicians. Half-hidden in the forest behind, other dragons, animals, and birds watch to see if the Fool will follow his intuition and choose the right path for him, the one that leads to greater spiritual and magickal knowledge. This spirituality is symbolized by the spirals seen on the rocks. If the Fool allows the critical conscious mind to regain control, he will miss the correct path and wander off into the desert of materialism.

Divinatory Meaning

New and startling opportunities arrive that are completely out of the usual way you live your life. You are contemplating a decision to break with the old way and embrace a new path. You make sudden decisions that are unexpected by those close to you. You are filled with an urge to investigate magick and/or different spiritual issues. A new cycle or an unplanned change of directions is at hand.

1

The Magician

Self-control; learning magick.

The Magician

The Fool has progressed far enough to see results from magickal studies and endeavors, thus becoming a practicing alchemical Magician. As the Magician stands before the altar, her concentration and actions have attracted many astral dragons to aid and guide. The dragon-topped wand in her left hand symbolizes the connection with the subconscious and superconscious minds, a vital and necessary ingredient to successful magick. Twining, green, Celtic embroidery on the robe reveals the awareness that the spiritual and physical must be balanced for progress along the path, and that all things in the physical and astral planes are intertwined. Psychic abilities are beginning to flourish, as seen in the half-formed images of dragons in the incense smoke. Using the dragon-topped wand, the Magician is focusing her attention on dragon energy and knowledge in order to comprehend the ancient wisdom in the book.

Divinatory Meaning

You are discovering how to use the laws of magick, faith, and willpower to get what you need and desire. Study and practice in a new career or spiritual path that attracts you. Your thoughts and energies flow in harmony to accomplish what needs to be done. This is an excellent time to gain self-control.

2

High Priestess

Unknown future.

High Priestess

The Magician has taken the important next step in her progress: that of initiation into the responsibility of a true magician. As a High Priestess, she has learned that each magician is responsible for any magick she or he does. She stands evenly positioned between a dragon of Light and a dragon of Chaos, striving to keep perfect balance so that magickal knowledge, spiritual growth, and life itself will be as positive and free of negative human emotions as is possible. There is a growing understanding of the need for both Goddess and God, female and male, or positive and negative energies. The crescent moon on her forehead symbolizes the cycles of life through which the changing world must go. The wand is topped with a small personal dragon, symbol of the magician's connection with Otherworlds and the powers there. Even though glimpses of the future in the crystal ball may be startling, the High Priestess faces the truth with calmness and inner wisdom. She feels the strength of the dragons all around and draws upon their ancient knowledge for guidance.

Divinatory Meaning

Hidden influences are at work; the future is in the process of being formed and is not jelled enough yet to fully predict. Ancient mystical knowledge or practical information comes your way. This phase of your life is an appropriate time to practice developing intuition and psychic abilities, to be more introspective. This is an excellent time to make new goals or refine the old ones.

3

The Empress

Unexpected blessings; Goddess influence.

The Empress

The pregnant Empress is in reality the Lady of Dragons, one who communicates strongly with dragons and patiently waits to give birth to new things, just as the dragon with her patiently hatches her eggs. These new things may be the result of magickal spellworkings, conscious goal-planning, or spiritual striving. The red robe is the warm color of vibrant life; the designs of eternal Celtic twinings, stars, and moons symbolic of the interconnectedness of everything in the Universe. As the Empress gazes up at the dragon, she laughs with sudden happiness and realization that she has a friend to help her on her astral journeys. This aid will extend to her magickal endeavors and everyday life itself. The Empress holds a bouquet of red roses, symbols of new cycles in life and rebirth of the self as the Empress learns more spiritual and magickal knowledge. The small dragon on her shoulder is her companion and familiar, her intermediary with all things astral. Its green color symbolizes growth, prosperity, and renewal.

Divinatory Meaning

Unexpected gifts and blessings come to you. A possible marriage or commitment to a relationship is close. You may experience a possible pregnancy, or period of creativity. Travel, pleasant recreation, or social gathering will benefit you at this time. Financial security and good fortune can be yours with planning and commitment. Goddess influences are at work in your life.

4

The Emperor

Power; God influence.

The Emperor

The Emperor, or Lord of Dragons, is powerful in his calmness and comprehension of universal laws and universal connectedness of all creation. As with his companion dragon, the Emperor's third eye sees both the physical and astral entities and energies around him. The brown of his tunic and trousers reveals his common sense attitude toward all things, but this is tempered and refined by the spiritual gold of the designs of his jewelry and clothing. He accepts the responsibility of his position on the spiritual path he has chosen, as he watches over and regulates the activities of the children (the power in the mystical center of each human) and the little dragons (newly formed magickal endeavors). The stars of his crown symbolize spiritual guidance through the labyrinth to spiritual oneness, both for himself and for others who might follow him. The long sword at his side represents the leadership and justice he must be prepared to render if necessary. He and his companion dragon sit peacefully in the beautiful garden of regeneration and renewal, the hidden spiritual place that is the goal of all seekers.

Divinatory Meaning

Your life will be smoother if you cultivate leadership and stability in order to progress. You may be influenced by a charismatic personality. You may move into a position of power in your job. This is a good time for real estate transactions. God influences come into your life. If in a negative position, this card indicates either a desire to control others or that you are being controlled.

5

High Priest

Facing karmic issues.

High Priest

The High Priest has studied long to gain the knowledge he now has. Like the High Priestess, he has learned to balance positive and negative energies, as symbolized in the tapestry of black and white dragons, and can channel a mixture of these potent powers to create and manifest. However, his realm of learning is applied more to the physical world and physical laws that benefit all humanity. His white tunic and gold trousers signify his position as a judge and intermediary. The blue cloak with gold trim represents the High Priest's spiritual connection with God and Goddess energies. The staff in his left hand, twined with green vines, shows his ability to draw upon astral and spiritual knowledge, while he directs his will through the crystal-topped wand in his right hand. He has moved beyond desiring to use will for selfish means and has entered the realm of balance in all things for the good of all upon the Earth. The tiny, dark gray dragon that sits on top of the wand is his companion and familiar, his guide into the astral realms when he travels there to gain more wisdom and knowledge.

Divinatory Meaning

Abide by the physical and spiritual rules, or suffer the consequences. A situation may require you to make a promise or sign a contract; read everything carefully, especially the fine print, and be certain you understand the terms. An inner spiritual teacher makes him/herself known. Dreams and visions in meditation or events in life itself make you face up to your responsibilities.

6

The Lovers

An emotional decision.

The Lovers

A Forest dragon stands on the bank of a lake, its neck outstretched to touch noses with a beautiful Water dragon that rises from the waters. They gaze at each other in love, unconcerned that their attraction will prove difficult because of their very different lifestyles. For the moment, they are caught up in the power of emotions. The Forest dragon represents the linear, analytical left brain and the conscious mind, while the Water dragon symbolizes the creative, spiritually connected right brain and the subconscious mind. To achieve success and reach goals, both halves of the brain, as well as the conscious and subconscious minds, must live and work together in harmony in order to reach a spiritual balance point. However, because of the vast differences in perceiving life and spirit, this is extremely difficult to maintain on a constant basis. Thus, we go through life in a kind of dance, approaching, then retreating from the balance point. The heron, representing generation of life, and the butterfly, symbolizing the soul itself, reveal that we must always be aware of the soul and its needs to grow, regardless of our emotional side-paths.

Divinatory Meaning

A romantic encounter may come into your life. You may be faced with an attraction or a temptation that may not be good for you. There will be an attraction of opposites that will be difficult to reconcile in the long run. A difficult choice will arise; make your decision on the facts, not the emotions.

7

The Chariot

Maintaining balanced control.

The Chariot

High on a mountain peak, two powerful dragons hold a large, sparkling crystal ball between them. Although of different elements and natures, they are firmly balanced and in harmony with each other. The positive and negative forces they control flow evenly into the atmosphere around them. The smaller dragons represent life-events that are attracted to this harmonious balance; events that seek the balance and harmony necessary for resolution. The high mountains are the gateway to the spiritual realm. Climbing them is a strenuous endeavor, one requiring commitment and determination. However, at the peak, when we at last rediscover our spiritual connections, we will also find the harmony and balance that our souls seek.

Divinatory Meaning

Balanced control of a situation allows you to benefit. Success comes through confidence and being centered. You must pull two opposing forces together to accomplish a goal.

8

Strength

Courage; inner strength.

Strength

A large dragon sits with its wings outstretched, its mouth open and emitting a controlled gust of fire. This dragon symbolizes the Guardian of the Threshold, the inner spiritual guardian who tests all initiates before they pass on to a higher level of spiritual development. The dragon challenges the seeker, but she is not afraid. She lifts her hand to it in love and understanding and stares into its eyes as she telepathically communicates her right to make this journey and pass through to greater achievements. Her willpower is strong, and she is determined to continue her quest. In her right hand is a red rose, representing her accomplishments. Her green robe is decorated with spirals, showing her conscious understanding of the constantly moving energies of creation-destruction, the very foundation of magick and growth. The green pentacles on her yellow gown reveal her connection with the Goddess and the protection derived from this connection. Her feet are bare on the dark stones; her foundation in the spiritual is secure and unimpeded. Several small dragons cluster about her feet, symbolic of her astral guides and teachers.

Divinatory Meaning

Let your intuition guide you in taking a stand. If you are right in a disagreement, do not give in, but use calm persuasion to carry you to victory. Use courage, willpower, and inner strength to overcome difficulties.

9

The Hermit

Solitude.

The Hermit

A large, very ancient dragon sits alone on a mountain ledge, a cave opening barely seen behind it. It is serenely studying an ancient book held open by its front claws. Another book and scrolls can be seen close to its side. The hermit dragon has deliberately sought solitude, for it knows that only when the conscious mind becomes quiet does true spiritual guidance make itself known and true understanding come. Spirals, representing the constantly moving energies of creation-destruction, can be seen in the rocks (foundation and stability of spiritual growth). Faint dragon and human faces in the stones symbolize the subtle but constant presence of teachers from the astral realms. These half-concealed faces also represent past lives we have experienced to reach our present place in time. This ancient dragon knows that, like the twisted tree and tangle of roots around it, life's path is seldom straight and easy to follow.

Divinatory Meaning

This card may represent a loner or one who prefers periods of solitude. A counselor or teacher gives you sound advice. Rethink your goals after giving the situation much thought; use all practical resources to come to your decision. Pull back from your frantic round of activities or your health and happiness may be harmed.

10

The Wheel

Change of fortune.

The Wheel

A large ancient book, entitled *The Grimoire of Life*, is held open by the claws of a dragon. One of the pages reveals a large eight-spoke Celtic wheel, an ancient symbol that all life turns and returns in patterns, cycles, and seasons. This symbolic message is repeated in the text: "The Wheel turns. Learn to ride with dragons." The triform spiral below the text is the Celtic symbol of fate, similar to the interlocked motif of three triangles that represented the Norse Fate Goddesses, the Norns. Dragons represent the flow of diverse and recycling energies throughout all creation and lives. When the Wheel turns, and we return to a certain pattern of energy and action, we call it karma. Karma can be positive or negative, paying or receiving, going forward or going backward. If we can learn the lesson embedded in "negative" karma, we can transform it into "positive" and move into a different cycle. However, we must be aware of truth (the feather quill) and be willing and diligent in seeking dragon-knowledge of universal energy flows if we are to succeed in our forward path through life.

Divinatory Meaning

Luck and fate are turning in your favor. Your life has entered a change of cycles that will allow you to move forward or slide backward, depending upon your preparation and determination. It is time to make changes. Break with incompatible lovers, friends, relationships, or careers.

11

Justice

Legal matters.

Justice

A large white dragon sits on a rocky path, with a forest close behind. On its head it wears a crown and in one paw it holds a scepter. In the other paw it holds an unrolled scroll (karmic records). Stern but majestic, the dragon will not be moved until the man and woman who stand before it have heard the reading of their karma and the spiritual justice this majestic dragon will dispense. The white dragon is a pure, unbiased spiritual being, the subconscious part of each of us that subtly demands that we acknowledge and live by adherence to spiritual laws. We may think we have skirted any retribution of the flaunting of such laws, but somewhere along our path we will discover that we can no longer move forward without facing the consequences of past actions or inactions. The dragon's gold crown symbolizes spiritual enlightenment, its scepter the willpower to make changes. The forest behind it represents the events of every life a human has lived and the mental and emotional qualities of the mind derived from those lives. All those who wish to go forward into a smoother life must accept the challenge of this dragon.

Divinatory Meaning

There is a possibility of encounters with lawyers, judges, or the police. Only logical thinking and facts will enable you to move forward. There can be a satisfactory conclusion to a legal matter if you take care. This card may herald the signing of contracts or legal papers.

12

The Hanged Man

Suspended activity.

The Hanged Man

A man hangs upside down over a deep, rocky chasm, one foot tangled in a vine. He is making no effort to free himself. He has forgotten that magick or change does not work alone, but requires his action and purpose. He makes no effort to touch the rocks, the source of primordial power and energy. Behind him, a waterfall (universal possibilities of primal matter) provides protection should he fall, but he is afraid to trust in spirit and the knowledge he has learned. Frightened of making a mistake, the man does nothing. He hangs suspended in a dangerous position, hoping that someone will rescue him, thereby taking away the need for a decision. All over the edges of the chasm and on the jutting rocks sit many kinds of dragons, large and small, watching what he will do. They are waiting to help him rise above this predicament if he would but reach out to them. Representing the elemental forces and energies that can be called upon and used in magick and willpower, the dragons wait patiently for the man to realize the solution to his problem is within reach and within himself.

Divinatory Meaning

A challenge to the way you think and live is coming. A period of inaction signals a need for introspection and rethinking of goals. Keep your feet on the ground and do not be taken in by illusions. Everything is in suspension and not moving, perhaps because of your inability to make a decision.

13

Death

Transformation.

Death

A large dragon is shedding its black skin and scales, emerging in a new identity of sparkling white. Its wings are spread in triumph and its head thrown back in a roar as it completes the successful transformation. Out of dark, stormy clouds comes a bright beam of sunlight, which illuminates the moment of victory. What was perhaps looked upon as a painful death or great loss has been revealed as a rebirth into something better. Knowledge, willpower, and trust in spirit have helped to create gold out of dross. Like the fabled Phoenix, the dragon rises from the symbolic ashes of an outworn existence or experience into a new and brighter cycle of life.

Divinatory Meaning

A significant transformation approaches. An unplanned event requires you to make a dramatic or radical change. Illusions are stripped away, leaving you with only the bare truth. A possible inheritance or unexpected money may come your way.

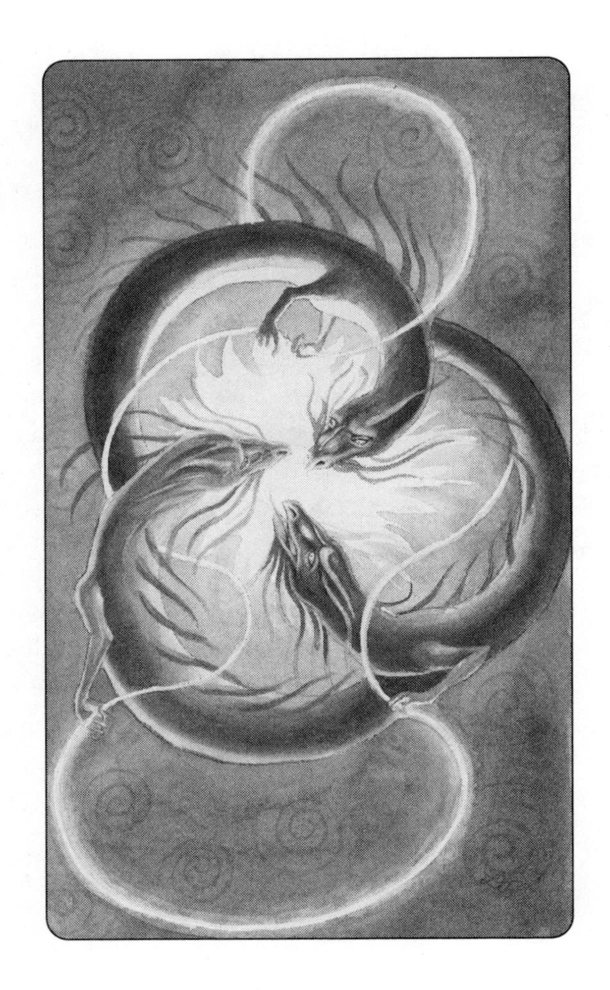

14

Temperance

New *perspectives*.

Temperance

In perfect harmony, three dragons coil and turn through the skies, weaving strands of spiritual energy with their claws. The sky itself holds repeating patterns of spirals, symbolizing the primal matter of creation-destruction that is all around us. One dragon is blue; another is shades of red; the third, shades of green. Red symbolizes vibrant life energies and the sexual drive; green, the productiveness of the mind; blue, the watery instability of emotion. All these must be twined together in equal parts in order to temper and modify life experiences, so that what is out-of-balance (intemperate) can be corrected. An elongated, golden lemniscate (a figure eight) of eternal life twines through the spinning circle of dragons, representing that a balanced life cannot exist without the important element of spirit.

Divinatory Meaning

This card may presage a period of creative inspiration, or a time of harmony and peacefulness. Self-control and inner guidance will get you through difficulties. A trip gives you a new perspective on an old issue. You need to adapt to new circumstances.

15

Chains

Oppressive situations.

Chains

A man and a woman stand chained together in a gloomy dungeon. A place of illusion, this dungeon is of their own making through ill-conceived action, inaction, wrong choices, and negativity. Although a brilliant beam of spiritual light shines upon them, they are so immersed in their own self-pity that they refuse to see that their freedom is at hand. Behind them, a Chaos dragon holds the chain in its claws. Believing Chaos to only be a negative state, the couple have allowed themselves to sink into despair, deliberately unaware that the chain is now broken. They refuse to acknowledge the sparks of light that fly from the ends of the broken chain, broken by the very chaotic conditions they fear. They do not call upon the powers of life and positive energy so close to them, symbolized by the color of their clothing. Instead, they stand with closed eyes, refusing to move away from their place of captivity, their source of pain and despair.

Divinatory Meaning

Fear or reluctance to break from a bad situation or relationship is hindering your progress. You are chained in an oppressive situation by refusing to see the truth. Someone is bullying or riding roughshod over you. Your energy is being wasted in indulgences. A relationship in which you are involved is based on the wrong reasons and is not productive. Untrustworthy people are presenting themselves as something other than they are.

16

The Tower

Discord; catastrophe.

The Tower

Two black Chaos dragons curl around a disintegrating stone tower. Their claws are tearing at the tower, and they breathe fire. The tower (in this instance, symbolic of the overblown human ego, vaunting pride, and refusal to take action on a circumstance) is being ripped apart by chaotic conditions created by imbalances in physical life and spiritual growth. Pieces of the tower are falling; other pieces litter the rocky ground. What was once thought to be of great importance is now destroyed. The dark sky is filled with storms, and lightning flashes. There is always spiritual light in the midst of unpleasant lessons if one will change perspective and look for it. Half-formed images of other dragons can barely be seen diving in and out of the storm clouds. Symbolic of primordial energy, these half-seen dragons can be coaxed into positive formation through effort, willpower, and looking at the truth.

Divinatory Meaning

You witness or experience a shocking event that leaves you changed. Potential catastrophe is near; be prepared. Your life is complicated by discord in a relationship or the family. Unforeseen setbacks bring despondency and a period of frustration. Your dreams may disintegrate into ashes.

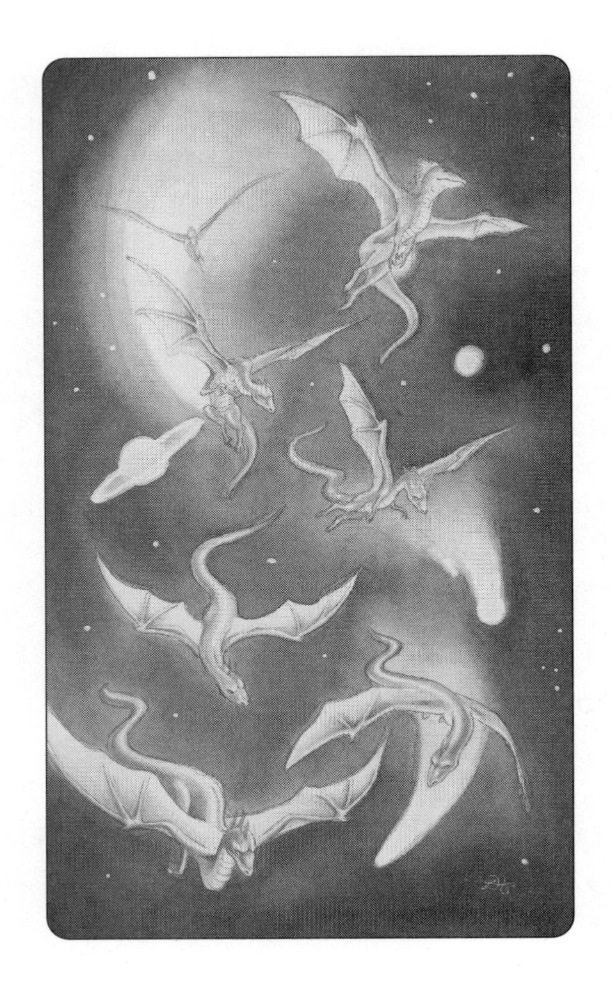

17

The Star

Spiritual experiences.

The Star

Seven golden-red dragons do a star dance through the night sky. There are stars all around them. The stars are beacons to guide the seeker through the journey of the subconscious and on to the path to a better physical and spiritual life. Shooting stars flash by, symbols of quickly moving events. The seeker must constantly keep alert in order to benefit from rapidly appearing and disappearing opportunities, some of which may never come again in this lifetime. Planets can be seen, including Jupiter with its rings, representing the positive energy and manifestations that can go hand-in-hand with certain opportunities and actions. The dragons ride the universal currents of unseen energy, instinctively knowing they are there to be used by those who know of their existence. Once the human seeker learns of the unlimited, invisible streams of universal power, he/she need only trust to instinct to call upon their boundless energy.

Divinatory Meaning

Personal spiritual experiences give you a glimpse of universal consciousness. You need to stretch beyond what you think is your potential. New opportunities will present themselves to you. Divine guidance is available if you listen.

18

The Moon

Dreams; intuition.

The Moon

A silvery-white dragon is engaged in a celestial dance with a Full Moon behind her. Her sacred dance creates and raises energy in preparation for magick or manifestation. The dragon dances atop a tangle of roots in a barren landscape, symbolic of creating purpose out of chaos, reality out of illusion, harmony out of discord. However, the dragon's steps are precise, her knowledge vast. She has left nothing to chance, neither does she allow herself to be tricked by half-truths. If done without a clear, definite purpose, energy raised magickally from the phases of the Moon produces illusionary power, deceitful images, and daydreams fed by foundationless imagination. The tangles of past lives (the roots under the dragon) have wandered aimlessly in their restless search for gratification without long-term goals. They exist in a barren landscape, devoid of color or life. To break the hold these lives exert upon the present, the magician must dance upon them until he/she sees only the truth behind each one. In the dark sky can be seen ancient Celtic and Pagan symbols.

Divinatory Meaning

Dreams, intuition, and/or psychic experiences will come unexpectedly. This is a time when you act on impulse without thinking things through. People who deal in illusion are drawn into your circle. Secret enemies are at work. Your negative and illusionary thinking are disrupting your progress. You feel victimized. Deceptions are being used against you.

19

The Sun

Positive Events.

The Sun

A large golden-red Fire dragon sweeps in and out of the Sun's flares, his fiery breath forming magickal symbols. He has learned to control the dangerous and unpredictable element of Fire, symbolized by the flaming Sun. What began for him as a painful lesson in endurance now has transformed into great benefits. Vast currents of energy rise about him, yet he freely rides the air currents as he draws upon this power to create and manifest his desires. His great scales, hardened by repeated excursions into this element, glisten and glow with power. This Fire dragon and his bravery symbolize what humans call "trial by fire," the tempering of the body, mind, and spirit through harsh, difficult events. Without enduring some "trials by fire," humans could not fully appreciate the positive side of life and the rewards of endurance and perseverance. Trailing behind the large dragon are two smaller Fire dragons.

Divinatory Meaning

Positive happenings leave you with a sense of freedom and joy. You may be blessed with material gain or recognition for your work. Good news is coming.

20

Judgment

Renewal; karmic issues.

Judgment

A large dragon tenderly administers healing and comfort to the man in the bed. Around his neck hangs a medallion with a triple spiral, symbol of life, death, and rebirth. As the man struggles with the mental and emotional agony that accompanies all cycles of renewal, the dragon looks on with love and understanding. The tracery on the window behind the dragon represents the Celtic Tree of Life, a symbol of the totality of all lives past, present, and future. The dragon's spring-green color represents rebirth, a condition all humans must experience if they are to progress into a higher realm of consciousness. It is the man's responsibility to awaken from the nightmare of illusion and despair, the haunting dream of helplessness. Help is there in the form of the dragon and brilliant sunlight if only the man would open his eyes and reach out.

Divinatory Meaning

Something or someone out of the past comes back into your life with influences you may or may not like. Handle karmic relationships or issues correctly or pay the price. This card may point to a change of home or job. You are attracted to a new line of spiritual or magickal study. You will face an unpleasant but necessary decision.

21

The World

Achieving success and goals.

The World

Two magicians, one male, one female, stand confidently with dragon-topped wands in their hands. They have completed the seeker's journey from The Fool to The World, a long and arduous task, but one that has benefited them in every way—physically, materially, emotionally, mentally, and spiritually. By learning how to work with the energy of the dragons and the Elements, they have learned to connect with everything in the Universe. They have discovered the great truth, that everything is connected on all planes of existence and in all realms. With their wands (willpower) they can receive from and send manifestation energy to any place or any creature, even across time. The misty sky around them holds Celtic symbols, such as spirals (unending primordial matter) and spinning wheels (movement of energy). These are faintly seen in the darkness, along with many stars (spiritual guides and teachers) and the bright forms of dragons (the ability to conquer all obstacles).

Divinatory Meaning

Everything is going right for you. You are contemplating a decision to cut away all the dead wood and begin a new cycle in life. This is a good time to achieve your goals. You are entering a period of success in all areas of your life. New opportunities arise.

Chapter 4

Minor Arcana

The Minor Arcana cards represent the details of each step in each cycle of life. They fill out and clarify the small details of a card position or of any Major Arcana card around which they fall. Where the Major Arcana cards are like the large cities on a map, the Minor Arcana cards are the roads that lead from one city to another.

Ace of Wands

New beginnings; new cycles.

Ace of Wands

Baby dragons are hatching out of a crystal nest in the clouds. A crystal-topped wand is visible in one of the babies' claws. One of the babies is fully hatched; another almost hatched; a third one can be seen with just the eyes visible through a hole in the shell. In the background a rainbow is coming out of stormy-looking clouds. The crystal nest is a symbol of the internal "hatching ground," the subconscious place where desires and ideas come together to produce the energy and enthusiasm needed to manifest material results. The crystal-topped wand represents concentrated spiritual energy, the last and most important ingredient to the manifestation. Crystal reflects all the colors of the rainbow when light is shone through it. The rainbow, both in the crystals and in the clouds behind the baby dragons, is the bridge between the material and etheric worlds. Humans frequently find themselves in different stages of accepting and implementing new ideas. Some receive the ideas with enthusiasm, while others are still struggling to break free of the restrictions of old cycles of life. Still others are afraid to expose themselves to the new experiences.

Divinatory Meaning

New beginnings are now possible. This is a good time to start a new cycle of life. Fresh ideas come to you from unexpected sources. An adventure is on the horizon.

Two of Wands

Focus will and energy.

Two of Wands

A man holds a crystal-topped wand in each hand, his arms stretched upward toward two Air dragons, one hovering on each side of him above. The man stands in a grassy, flower-studded meadow with mountains behind him. Near his feet are small sacred stones carved with Celtic spirals. These spiral designs are repeated in the pattern on his vest. The two wands, or scepters, symbolize the man's ability and willpower to harness both positive and negative energies to make changes in his life. This is essential, as both types of energy are needed for balance and manifestation. The two hovering dragons are another emblem of the female-male, positive-negative energies. The spirals in both the rocks and his clothing represent the constantly moving, inexhaustible energies of the Universe. He has found his way through a series of spiritual gateways (the mountains) to this peaceful meadow of creativity (the three stones).

Divinatory Meaning

Focus your will and energy to accomplish your desires. Help with realization of a dream may come from a distance. A new endeavor requires courage and planning for the future.

Three of Wands

Planning; partnership.

Three of Wands

A crystal-topped wand is stuck in the ground on a little sand dune overlooking the ocean. Two Air dragons coil through the sky, a similar wand held by each. Flashes of light are coming from the wand in the sand up toward the wands held by the dragons. Here, the number three of creative inspiration and pure creativity is prominent. The dragons are positive and negative energies combining through a spiritual connection (the wand). The four Elements, so vital to all physical manifestations, are shown in the rocks and sand of the beach (Earth), the gently-rolling ocean (Water), the fiery flashes from the wands (Fire), and rainbow-colored sky (Air). Whatever plans are put into motion, whether magickal or mundane, require the four Elements. There must be thought (Air), an emotional involvement (Water), a degree of practicality (Earth), and action (Fire). If one Element is missing in the equation, there will be no manifestation.

Divinatory Meaning

Successful ideas require a period of planning to succeed. A partnership is possible in your work. Your business or career could either take you to or establish communications with distant places.

Four of Wands

Happiness; rest; success.

Four of Wands

A tall castle with a large square tower to the front sits in a rocky, forbidding setting. On three corners of the tower is a sparkling wand. A dragon, holding a fourth wand, perches on the top of this tower. Beside him are a young man and woman, their arms about each other. The castle is both fortification and home, a secure place where love and life can grow and the distressing problems of the world can be shut out for a time. Castles are frequently built in bleak landscapes of difficult lives (symbolized by the faces in the rocks). Still, the castles are beautiful to the inhabitants, and filled with peace and love. The storm clouds are breaking overhead, signaling the end of a difficult cycle in life. The dragon is both guardian and co-magician for the inhabitants.

Divinatory Meaning

Happiness and peace are now within your grasp. Your past endeavors bring a well-earned rest from cares. A new love is now possible. Success may give you a reason to celebrate.

Five of Wands

Obstacles; opposition.

Five of Wands

Five robed magicians (some men, some women) are battling each other with their wands. Flashes of magickal energy come from the wands, as the magicians either defend themselves or attack others. These magicians represent two types of people in the world: those who are overly ambitious and jealous of what others accomplish, and those who must learn to defend themselves against such attacks by others. Jealous people often attack those who have worked hard and gained positive things from their efforts; unfortunately it is a common human failing. Life is difficult enough (symbolized by the rocky landscape and twisted tree roots), without complicating it with unnecessary battles brought on by misunderstandings, jealousy, and twisted ethics. Only a cool head, spiritual guidance, and resistance to foes will help a balanced person win the day. Tiny Air dragons dart above them, their fiery breath intermingling with the flashes of energy. They represent the astral guardians who try to bring peace to such a situation.

Divinatory Meaning

Obstacles and opposition from others may complicate your life; you will have to struggle to overcome this. Harmful gossip could damage your reputation and/or career. You may find yourself in trouble with the law.

Six of Wands

Success after hard work.

Six of Wands

A woman with a small dragon on her shoulder stands with a crown on her head. A five-point star is centered on her forehead, directly over the spiritual third eye. This symbolizes the woman's connection with spiritual guidance and her access to ancient knowledge. Before her is a table covered with rolled scrolls, quill pens, and other magickal equipment. Prominently to the front is a brass vase holding six crystal-topped wands. Other small dragons fly and sit about the room. The star (pentacle of protection and symbol of the Goddess) and the crown (spiritual enlightenment) reveal that this magician is on a higher path of life. She has gathered her willpower (the wands) and placed them in a position to bring about fertility and manifestation (the vase). This fertile energy is repeated in the Celtic scrollwork carved into the table, the magician's center for working her will.

Divinatory Meaning

You are rewarded with success after hard work. A message of good news brightens your day. There could be an advancement in career. Supportive friends give you the courage to follow your dreams.

Seven of Wands

Difficulties; competition.

Seven of Wands

A huge Air dragon coils protectively about a woman holding a bright Celtic sword. The woman is not a novice (a young person), but a mature magician who has experienced life and learned to fight the necessary battles. She knows well the availability of universal energy (the spirals on her dress and arm-guards) and the power of manifestation (the vine decorations on her bodice). All energy moves constantly, from the outer rim to the center and back again. The stylized Tree of Life on her belt represents her connection with the dark, mysterious subconscious mind. The dragon has a wand in its mouth, a symbol of necessary willpower to accomplishment a goal. Six other similar wands are arranged upright like a barrier before the dragon and woman. The faint pyramid-shaped scales on the dragon's head symbolize the Cosmic Light that is necessary for regeneration. Confident in her own ability to tap into universal energy and the protection offered her by both her astral companion (the dragon) and willpower (wands), the woman stands firm against aggression.

Divinatory Meaning

This card points to difficult times ahead. Competition in something important to you will bring difficulty and harsh feelings. Be aware and protect yourself against adversaries. Now is the time to take a stand on an issue that is important to you.

Eight of Wands

Movement; urgency.

Eight of Wands

Eight dragons fly across the deep, mysterious void of a cosmic sky, each one holding a crystal-topped wand. Starlight flashes off the crystal tips of the wands. The stars are spiritual beacons that guide those who journey through life. Oftentimes, those on a life-journey feel as if they are in a bottomless void, with no direction to guide them out of the situation. That is the time to call upon your personal dragon guardians, look within for spiritual direction, and use your willpower (wand) to find your way to your goal.

Divinatory Meaning

Barriers fall and events move quickly. Urgent messages of a positive nature come your way. You may take a journey, possibly by air.

Nine of Wands

A Pause.

Nine of Wands

A man holding a wand stands between two large Air dragons. His expression is one of tiredness but triumph. The magician has moved through many trials and tribulations to reach this moment of rest and success. Behind him is a dark, twisted wood, the frightening and mysterious depths of the subconscious, where malicious faces of past lives or past experiences in this life may rise to haunt him. To succeed in his journey, he had to acknowledge past errors and build upon that experience. A steep stair leads back from where he stands into the woods, symbolizing that his journey through this life is not yet finished. However, at this moment he and the dragons stand in full sunlight, representing spiritual power. In a semicircle above the man's head are eight wands, their tips flashing in the sunlight. If he can keep his willpower bright, he can ascend the steps without worry.

Divinatory Meaning

There is a pause in a difficult lifecycle, giving you a much needed rest. This is a time when you must carefully plan your next step. Success is in sight but more effort is needed.

Ten of Wands

Struggle; loss.

Ten of Wands

A dragon sits on a mountain peak with ten wands held under one of his feet. A woman pulls herself up the steep slope, over the rocks, toward the dragon. She is tired but determined. Her face is lifted to the dragon waiting above her. The woman is willing to go through a difficult life-journey to learn the key to success from her astral guardian. The wands are the key, for they symbolize concentrated willpower, a necessary trait which the dragon will help her to achieve. She bears the marks of her journey over every rock (stability and foundation) she has climbed as she struggles higher into the mountains (the gateway to spiritual learning). Her eyes fastened on the dragon, she never loses sight of her goal, no matter how difficult the journey. The dragon's companionship and encouragement keeps her from giving up.

Divinatory Meaning

You have to struggle to keep things going. A difficult series of events taxes your strength and endurance. You will experience a minor but painful loss after much effort.

Page of Wands

Important news; foreign places.

Page of Wands

A young girl stands beside a small Guardian dragon, her face bright and smiling, one hand on the dragon's head. She is completely without fear. As an innocent, trusting child, she demonstrates the necessary qualities to finding and befriending astral guides and companions. She holds a wand (willpower) in one hand and a rolled scroll (ancient knowledge learned through spiritual connection) is tucked under one arm. The dragon is smiling in contentment at the telepathic communication of love, the ancient and successful method of contacting anyone and anything in the other planes of existence, as well as in spirit. From the dragon's wings come sparkles of magickal energy. By the dragon and little magician working together, access to creative energy is much easier.

Divinatory Meaning

A message that gives hope comes at a crucial time. You receive important news that relates to your job or field of studies. Some phase of your job or social activities brings you into contact with foreign countries or people.

Knight of Wands

Sudden changes.

Knight of Wands

A teenage boy sits astride an Air dragon as it flies through the air. A sword hangs at his side, and he wears a shiny breastplate, boots, and blue trousers and shirt. In a pouch hanging from one shoulder you can see the end of a wand. The young magician has progressed beyond simple communication with his teachers and has learned to become a Dragon Rider, one who has greater access to creative energies. He knows the value of astral travel for spiritual growth and a happier life. Because of his trust in his dragon companion, the magician will not come to harm, as long as he listens to words of advice. The void between worlds is a place where positive and negative energies are in balance, there is complete harmony and peace and a seeming sense of nothingness. Yet the void (between the worlds or within oneself) contains perfection, a oneness with all life forms everywhere.

Divinatory Meaning

There is a possibility of a sudden change of residence or job. Quick action is needed to resolve some issues in your favor. Things are now moving forward.

Queen of Wands

Reaping rewards; social events.

Queen of Wands

A royal-looking older woman stands near a throne of rich wood carved with Celtic symbols, a wand in one hand. She wears a crown with a blue stone in the front. A huge, dark blue dragon coils from behind the throne, its head near her feet. In a large, open window to one side, strange coils of clouds can be seen. On the back of the throne and on the window ledge sit a number of smaller hand-sized dragons. This queen, the Mistress of Air, has earned the right to her throne through her studies, her trials in life, and her calmness to face whatever lies ahead. Her entire wand (willpower) glows with directed purpose. The bag at her waist represents her vast accumulation of spiritual wealth. The spirals on her gown symbolize the unlimited cosmic energy she has learned to control and direct, according to her will and goals. Beyond the window, and her life, events may seem chaotic. However, she maintains a center of calm. Her jewels represent rewards for her struggles and perseverance.

Divinatory Meaning

A feminine influence, who is socially active, could aid you in some way. You achieve success in a goal. A round of social activities brightens your life. This is a time for reaping good rewards from your labors.

King of Wands

Ambition; leadership.

King of Wands

A regal-looking older man sits on a richly carved throne; he wears a crown with small blue stones on the spiky tips. Because of the man's long and dedicated studies, he has earned the title of Master of Air. Chaotic thoughts no longer plague him, for he has become disciplined in weeding out, organizing, and bending the power of those thoughts to his concentrated desire and goals. About his shoulders is a white and multiblue mantle (comfort and contentment), with tiny dragon figures as part of the design. On one partially raised hand sits a tiny, dark blue dragon, a small messenger that helps the king to communicate with other realms. The king's other hand holds a long staff-like wand (willpower) with a crystal tip; its glow shows the purity of his will. A huge dragon peers over the back of the throne above the man's head. This is the king's guardian and advisor, a long-time companion on journeys through other realms of being. Another of his small Guardian dragons lies curled contentedly at his feet, its sleep revealing the calmness of the atmosphere around this powerful man.

Divinatory Meaning

A masculine influence, who is powerful in the business world, could guide you in an important decision. Ambition and leadership qualities will get you ahead in your career. Beware that haste and ego do not get you into trouble.

Ace of Swords

Decisions; activity.

Ace of Swords

Baby Fire dragons are hatching out of a nest set among the lower fire vents on the slope of a volcano. A Celtic sword visible behind the nest stands upright and has carved dragons twining around the hilt. In the background the volcano is glowing and blowing smoke. The clouds are dark with reflections of fire on them. Fire symbolizes physical, mental, and spiritual strength and action. This strength can manifest either as destructive power or regeneration, depending upon the intent and self-discipline of the individual. The sword also has much the same meaning: strength and defense, the power to liberate or wound. Potential for self-destruction is represented by the active volcano in the background. Our lives are often disrupted by cataclysmic events, which sometimes seem to destroy our lives and turn them upside down. If we can learn to harness the fire of these events, we can walk safely through the flames and come out stronger than we were.

Divinatory Meaning

You are in the process of making decisions that will affect your life for some time. A new period or cycle of much activity is imminent. Beware of activity without thought.

Two of Swords

Tension; indecision.

Two of Swords

A Fire dragon holds two long swords in its claws, as it faces a man across an open, blazing vent in the rocky ground. The only connection to the other side is a narrow stone bridge without railings. The man hesitates, one foot on the bridge, one foot on the solid ground. One of his hands is outstretched to take a sword, but he must cross to get one. Celtic spirals are carved into the stark stones of the surrounding landscape. The bridge represents the link between the conscious and subconscious minds. This tenuous area of the mind can be a frightening place when one is learning to join the psychic senses with everyday, common-sense deductions in order to make better decisions. The only way to safely cross the bridge is to walk across without analyzing the potential for defeat or looking down at the dangerous fires below. The strength to take action can be drawn from knowledge of the meaning of the Celtic spirals; any momentary failure can be a stepping stone to a new opportunity.

Divinatory Meaning

There is tension and indecision in relationships or friendships. You are having difficulty gaining a sense of balance because you have no definite plans as to the direction you want to go. You are faced with having to balance two important things in life without being able to make a firm decision.

Three of Swords

Emotional upheavals.

Three of Swords

Three Fire dragons fight in a stormy sky above a blazing forest fire. Each holds a Celtic sword. They twist together in a Celtic knot. The number three was an ancient sacred number, denoting the Goddess and Her power of destruction and regeneration, death and rebirth. Here, the power is tangled and bound in a knot, signifying the stopping of progress. The swords of action are used for wounding, not liberating. The dragons are oblivious to the destruction caused by their dissension. The forest (events in life) has exploded into a destructive fire because of the wrong choice of action. Tangled in emotional anger, a person can fail to realize the destruction such feelings and actions bring to the rest of life.

Divinatory Meaning

Arguments and emotional upheavals will dominate this period of your life. There is a deep sense of loss and betrayal caused by someone close to you.

Four of Swords

Rest; a pause.

Four of Swords

A dragon rests on a rocky plain, its head outstretched. Even though its eyes are closed, all its senses are alert. Beside it a young woman lies sleeping against its massive body. Four ornate swords are laid out on the ground in front of the dragon, ready for use if need be. The landscape is rocky and stark, a symbol of the exhausting events that brought the woman and her dragon companion to this resting place. Their struggles and determination have earned them this respite. The woman is aware of the Celtic spirals of unlimited energy within the barren rocks themselves, energy that she can use to advance along her life-path when she is ready to proceed. The swords represent the four Elements, as well as strength and defense. With them, the woman will learn how to control psychic energy and manifest a better life for herself. By trusting in her astral dragon, she has established a clear line of communication with Spirit and her divine center of being.

Divinatory Meaning

This card heralds a time of rest after great anxiety and upset. There will be a pause before events move on to something better. You face a period of low physical energy.

Five of Swords

Slander; arguments; failure.

Five of Swords

Two men tug ferociously at the hilt of a sword, glaring at each other. They struggle in the open area before a stone mansion, symbolizing the best results of their lives. One of the men already has three other swords lying on the ground behind him and a sheathed sword at his belt. However, he is determined to take the other man's sword. Greed and vindictiveness have consumed him. He makes no effort to control his emotions and has convinced himself that it is his right to take what belongs to another. Tiny Fire dragons twist and flare in the air above the men, trying to stop the struggle and restore peace. Behind the men is a large, rearing dragon, its mouth open and flames shooting out. It bars the door to the mansion and will prevent the aggressor from enjoying his victory should he overcome his victim. Greed and knowledge misused will only bar the greedy man from happiness and contentment.

Divinatory Meaning

You face a period of malicious slander, arguments, and pettiness. There is a possibility of failure of plans. Problems and trouble may arise from rash behavior.

Six of Swords

Journeys; difficult choices.

Six of Swords

A woman stands with a pack on her back, a staff in one hand, and a sword slung at her belt. Beside her stands a large dragon with five other swords slung in a sheath around its neck. A tiny dragon sits on her shoulder, while on the other side of her sits a small Guardian dragon with a pack on its back. The woman and her dragon-friends look out over the hazy distance at a towering castle. Celtic spirals can be seen in the rocks about the woman. On her right ankle is a triform tattoo. With her strength and magickal authority (staff), the woman has crossed through a desolate landscape with her astral companions. She draws energy from the stones around her, knowing that she must ride with the tides of universal energy (the spirals). Her tattoo is a symbol of her power to banish what is not constructive to her life, while its triform shape indicates that she is balanced in body, mind, and spirit. Her goal is the spiritual center of all things, the castle.

Divinatory Meaning

A journey or move from one place to another is indicated. To progress you must make a change in consciousness and attitude. A difficult choice must be made that may involve great changes.

Seven of Swords

Bad feelings; snooping.

Seven of Swords

A man is carrying away seven swords from an opened chest just behind him. The lock on the chest is broken, so he is stealing what is not his. On a shelf above the chest, two tiny Fire dragons are screaming in anger. The little dragons try to warn him, but he refuses to listen. The thief has forced open the perilous box of universal, magickal knowledge within his subconscious mind and thinks to steal away with the power (swords) he found within. Only an initiate, who has studied and brought balance to all areas of his life, is given the key to open this perilous chest of wisdom and power. The thief has found a shortcut to gain what he wants without the work or dedication. He believes he is above the Law and will not suffer karmic consequences. However, he is wrong, for the Law will always be balanced, regardless of human desires to the contrary.

Divinatory Meaning

You are creating trouble through the wrong use of personal power. Failure of a plan may come about because of wrong motives. Do not snoop into the affairs of another; you will get burned. You feel cheated or wronged.

Eight of Swords

Restriction; fear.

Eight of Swords

A dragon is looking into a tower window at a young woman who is held captive inside. It waits patiently for the captive to see that escape is possible. It will give encouragement, but will not do what the woman could do for herself. The bars on the window, which do not fully cover the opening, are made of eight swords. Although these swords symbolize wounding, not liberating, they have not cut off the woman's retreat from the tower. The half-dead vines represent the dying fertility of the woman's life, the loss of her interconnectedness with all universal energy. The woman raises her bound hands toward the dragon, pleading for help. She has endured her captivity for so long, she no longer believes she can loosen the ropes that bind her, although the knots are simple and well within her reach. She pleads for outside help instead of taking action.

Divinatory Meaning

A turn of events or your own indecision leaves you feeling bound and restricted. You are afraid to leave an unpleasant relationship or job. There is the possibility of illness.

Nine of Swords

Great sadness; loss.

Nine of Swords

Two Fire dragons stand beside a man who is seated on a rock with his head in his hands. The man has wandered into a land of desolation, a place of mental, emotional, and spiritual poverty. His clothes (his physical life) are tattered, and he holds his head in despair. He is faced with the consequences of his past actions and karmic events. He is totally oblivious to the astral companions who keep watch over him. On the rocky ground beside him are nine broken swords, symbolizing his broken strength. The sky is brilliant with sunset colors, representing the life energy that could be his, if he would only look up and accept it. However, the man is so beaten down by his regrets and the events that brought him to this realization that he cannot see any way out of his predicament.

Divinatory Meaning

This card indicates a time of great misery, sadness, and depression. There could be a permanent loss or death of someone close to you. Severe illness is possible.

Ten of Swords

Disruption; dark times.

Ten of Swords

A large dragon lies on a hilltop, blood flowing from wounds in its side. Leaning against him is a woman warrior, a sword across her knees. She also is wounded, and her head droops in exhaustion. Nine sword blades point toward the woman and the dragon, symbolizing the present power of their enemies. The woman and her dragon companion have fought a good fight against the negative events of life, but are temporarily defeated, despite their courage and skills. However, there is hope, for behind them stand the ancient stones of strength and endless universal energy. They will rest and recover from their wounds, with their enemies seemingly triumphant for a time. Then the woman warrior and the dragon will draw upon deep reserves of energy from the four Elements and rise up to continue their spiritual journey.

Divinatory Meaning

You will experience a total disruption of plans and hopes. Bankruptcy may disrupt your life. Be prepared for a dark night of the mind and soul that may require counseling.

Page of Swords

Impulsiveness; troubles.

Page of Swords

A young boy holds up a tiny, baby Fire dragon on one hand, delight and fascination on his face. Behind him on the wall hangs a great Celtic sword and shield. At his feet lies a rolled scroll, symbolic of spiritual messages. However, the boy does not notice that a second baby Fire dragon has set fire to the scroll. Because of his inattention, he does not receive the message. The shield not only represents protection, but personal identity. Knights painted identifying marks on their shields so they would know friend from foe. The sword of strength and defense hangs ready for use. By allowing himself to become obsessed with his new discovery, the boy has failed to be aware of what happens around him. Small events (the second little dragon) can cause destruction if one does not remain alert.

Divinatory Meaning

You may have an impulsive desire for new experiences that could cause problems. Be warned of unexpected changes. This card is an advanced notice of a troubled period in life.

Knight of Swords

Misfortune; persecution.

Knight of Swords

A young woman, clad in a breastplate and helmet, rides a Fire dragon, sword upraised and a smile on her face. She has ridden the dragon very close to dangerous mountainsides and knife-like rocks. Her dragon is trying to avoid the rocks slicing so close to its wings. The woman is so consumed with the thrill of the wild ride that she risks both her dragon and herself needlessly. When one first learns to ride the power of astral energy (the dragon), one can become careless. Moving too quickly toward the limitless primordial power (the stones) and the gateway to the realm of spirit (the mountains) can have disastrous results. A little training does not make one proficient in controlling astral or psychic powers.

Divinatory Meaning

An unexpected misfortune could be near. There will be unforeseen attacks on you as a person. You could suffer persecution because of your religious beliefs; be careful sharing your views.

Queen of Swords

Learning lessons; manipulation.

Queen of Swords

The Queen of Swords is a mature woman who walks through a pit of fire with confidence. Although the flames flare around her on all sides, her face is calm, her eyes straight ahead. She has learned that life offers both positive and negative learning experiences and that one becomes stronger by refusing to give in to fear and despair. In one hand she carries a raised sword, while the other rests on the head of the large Fire dragon who is mostly hidden behind her and from whose mouth issues yet more flames. The sword represents the Queen's faith in her ability to fight her way through any adversity, while the huge dragon-companion symbolizes astral and spiritual teachers who are always beside us, not to impede our progress by making life too smooth, but to guide our steps through any "trial" to safety. The Queen wears a crown with a triangular-shaped, red stone in the front, symbolic of her connectedness with both the Goddess and her own feminine power. Three little Fire dragons frolic in the flames, encouraging her to continue her path.

Divinatory Meaning

This card indicates a powerful feminine influence. You will be faced with a period in your life that makes you learn an important lesson you have avoided. Be careful getting your way in something through manipulation, for later this action will come back to haunt you.

King of Swords

Opposition; obey the laws.

King of Swords

The King of Swords stands on a ledge inside a great underground cavern. The cavern is part of the interior of an active volcano, a place of primordial energy for either creation or destruction. In one hand the king holds a sword (his strength of will) as he stares down into the bubbling lava and fierce fire. He has studied long and hard to learn how to reach this divine, but potentially volatile, center of power within himself. Looking up at him out of this pit of roiling heat and molten rock is a large Fire dragon, with a baby on its shoulder. The king has learned through life experience that he must take responsibility for all his actions and uses of magickal energy. He has mastered self-control of his emotions, knowing when to defend and when to release. He knows he can now walk through fire and control his fear of unexpected events. His crown represents spiritual enlightenment, the result of a lifetime of searching. Behind him, up the flight of stairs, sits his massive throne, symbolic of stability and security. The king descended the stairs, deep into his subconscious mind, and now makes contact with universal, manifesting power, from which he will mold his desires into actuality.

Divinatory Meaning

This card suggests a powerful, but stubborn, masculine influence who may be opposing you. In a new project, do everything exactly by the rules or you will lose. There may be a need for the services of an attorney.

Ace of Cups

Joy; fertile period.

Ace of Cups

Baby dragons are hatching out of a nest floating on the waters of a gentle stream below a waterfall. One hatched baby is looking at her reflection in the water, while another leans contentedly against her. A third baby is struggling out of its shell, while a fourth is settling itself for a peaceful nap. All humans, at whatever stage of life, begin their seeking for spiritual and/or emotional growth and knowledge with the naivete and innocence of children. They are innocent of the difficulties and perils that may lie ahead and at the same time enthusiastic to get started on their journey. Some get caught up in admiring themselves and what they believe they can do, while others are content just to bask in the sunlight and lean on others. Still others struggle through obstacles and become stronger for this. This struggle is reflected in the faces on the rock. The waterfall and the chalice are symbolic of the endless stream of lives that proceed from and return to the Goddess and God.

Divinatory Meaning

New beginnings in your life will fill you with joy and contentment. Your spiritual growth will expand and take you to a higher level of understanding. There is the possibility of a new love. This card can also herald a possible pregnancy, so take care if this is not what you want. This can also foretell a fertile period for ideas.

Two of Cups

Love; friendship; commitment.

Two of Cups

A man and a woman stand in a small clearing, surrounded by ancient stones bearing Celtic spirals of unending life. Roses of achievement and perfection grow among stones, symbols of primordial power. The couple is holding a chalice between them, their eyes on each other. They are very happy for they have learned that sharing of balanced and loving emotions is the key to a successful relationship. Behind them is a Water dragon with a chalice held in its claws. With the Moon of spiritual discipline and initiation behind it, the dragon is pouring water from its cup into theirs, representing the flow of astral love, energy, and knowledge that comes to those who seek spiritual enlightenment.

Divinatory Meaning

A great love or friendship is now possible. This card can also indicate an engagement, marriage, or birth announcement. There is the necessity of a commitment of some kind.

Three of Cups

Prosperity; success.

Three of Cups

A Water dragon lies in a cave on a vast pile of treasure. Prominent in the front among the treasure are three chalices. Symbolic of the riches of spirit deep within the sacred center of each human, the dragon waits patiently to share this treasure with any who seek its realm. The treasure itself represents the hidden knowledge found within the subconscious and collective unconscious minds of all humans. The lapping water (the constant giving and receiving of emotional wealth) can be seen in the front of the card. Shimmering water reflections show on the cave walls, symbolic of the love and contentment that shine forth from the lives of all who are balanced and at peace.

Divinatory Meaning

A time of prosperity, success, good luck, and happiness is coming. A celebration may brighten your life. This can be a successful creative period.

Four of Cups

Old memories; dissatisfaction.

Four of Cups

A woman studies a chalice she holds in her hands. On the table before her sit three different chalices. The chalices are all empty; one is on its side, with water pouring out. The woman is completely lost in her memories, which she has reconstructed to suit her present frame of mind, but they are not real (the empty chalices). She has drained these memories of anything of value and not bothered to fill them again. She prefers to live in false dreams rather than become involved in life. Four tiny Water dragons sit and lie on the table, symbols of the love, companionship, and emotional abundance that could be hers if she would acknowledge them.

Divinatory Meaning

Stop dwelling on old memories. A relationship is tested. You are experiencing illogical dissatisfaction with a relationship or job; step back and look at the problem before taking any action.

Five of Cups

Negative events.

Five of Cups

A man is half-turned away from a richly covered table holding five chalices, some upright, some on their sides. One chalice is cracked, spilling its abundance onto the table. The man has become so blinded by illusions and falsehoods that he refuses to see the wealth of life and spirit he leaves behind him. Small dragons (symbols of his astral guides and teachers) flutter about his head, unnoticed. They are unable to change his fruitless course of action, for he has ceased to listen. The open door beyond him represents the blank unknown into which he goes without direction or aid.

Divinatory Meaning

You may be hurt from seeing through an illusion. This is a period when you tend to dwell only on negative events or happenings. This card foretells the possibility of a divorce or the breakup of a marriage or friendship. You may need to fight against a feeling of depression.

Six of Cups

Reunions; unexpected gifts.

Six of Cups

A little boy and girl are smiling and hugging two large Water dragons, who rise out of a pond. The children symbolize the natural psychic connection all humans possess before they are taught such a thing is false. They are freely communicating with astral creatures because it is a normal thing to do. On the flower and tree-covered banks stand six chalices. The flowers and trees represent constant renewal of life, fed by the waters of the lake (emotional purity and balance). Tiny dragons flutter happily around the children, symbols of the potential power of even the tiniest pieces of cosmic energy. The six chalices represent the power of building in all its connotations; building of realtionships, healing power, and bridges between people and/or species. By acknowledging this power of building, we acknowledge the interconnectedness of all things, animate and inanimate.

Divinatory Meaning

A reunion with old friends may be near. New opportunities present themselves; be ready to act on them. Unexpected gifts may surprise you.

Seven of Cups

Daydreams; responsibility.

Seven of Cups

A large Water dragon watches as a man stares up at a rocky ledge. This ledge holds seven chalices. One chalice holds jewels (prosperity); a second, a tiny misty castle (security); a third, a red heart (love); a fourth, a sword (protection); a fifth, a skull (dangerous adventures); a sixth, a wand and scroll (study and knowledge); and a seventh has a tiny Water dragon (astral guide to other realms) perched on its rim. The man has set no goals for himself, thus he is unable to make a choice. The dragon waits patiently for the man to ask for its aid, but the man is lost in daydreams where reality has no meaning.

Divinatory Meaning

You spend too much time daydreaming and not enough time taking action. Too many projects are going at once and not enough is done on any one. You refuse to look at reality.

Eight of Cups

Lack of discipline.

Eight of Cups

Two Water dragons watch as a woman walks away from eight jeweled chalices set on the bank of their lake. The woman wears a traveling cloak and has a pouch slung over one shoulder. In her despair, she looks beyond herself for fulfillment, thus journeying from place to place in search of happiness. This happiness can never exist or grow unless she is happy with herself. She turns her back upon the riches (chalices) offered by the Water dragons. These dragons know the secret of balanced emotions and contentment. However, the woman refuses to listen and moves away from the source of her help.

Divinatory Meaning

Goals are abandoned too soon. You do not discipline yourself to stick to any one thing. You have been, or are, refusing to take responsibility. Continuing to walk away from these responsibilities will only bring you more discontent and unhappiness.

Nine of Cups

Wishes granted.

Nine of Cups

A majestic Water dragon rises out of a lake with an ornate chalice full of jewels in its claws. A woman stands with outstretched hands to take the chalice. She has realized that she has the right to ask for help in attaining her goals, symbolized by the eight rich-looking chalices that sit around her feet on the shore. Abundance is unlimited, whether the abundance is spiritual growth, emotional contentment, physical health, or material possessions. The waves on the water symbolize the constant movement within the realm of universal possibilities.

Divinatory Meaning

Your wish will be granted. Success, accomplishment, and satisfaction will soon enter your life.

Ten of Cups

Goals reached; contentment.

Ten of Cups

A man and woman stand together with their two children, looking at a table that holds ten chalices. This abundance of chalices symbolizes the reward for their efforts to create a positive life. Coming from the chalices are rainbow lights, a reflection of their spiritual happiness and the balance of their emotions. Tiny Water dragons crawl in and out of a vase nearby, while others swoop through the air over the couple's heads. The dragons and their movements symbolize the constant flow of magickal energy. The boy and girl peek over the top of the table at the chalices, smiling at the abundance and the vibrant activities of the little dragons. A large, shadowy Water dragon is seen in the background. It represents the peace attained when emotions are in balance.

Divinatory Meaning

Goals are reached successfully. Contentment and happiness come into your life. Strong friendships or love brighten your existence. A joyful family occasion is possible.

Page of Cups

Message of love.

Page of Cups

The Page of Cups is a young girl who is standing beside a Water dragon that is partially submerged in a lake. The dragon and the lake represent the secret of controlling and using emotional energy. The clouds behind the dragon are divine forces overlooking the Page, her mission, and her life. In the dragon's mouth is a scroll decorated with an image of a chalice. The Page reaches for it, eager to receive this ancient knowledge, for she knows she must learn emotional control before she can advance on her spiritual path. Her companion and Guardian dragon sits near her, ready to help if she asks. The spiral shells and spiral markings on the rocks represent the constantly moving energies of creation, the universal movement that always leads to the center.

Divinatory Meaning

Fresh ideas and new methods of doing things make you more optimistic about your future. A message of love arrives. You receive a gift given in friendship.

Knight of Cups

Unexpected pleasant times.

Knight of Cups

The Knight of Cups, a teenage boy, is riding on a Water dragon across ocean waves. The Knight has not yet come into the fullness of his magickal and spiritual knowledge or experience. He is testing himself by pushing his ride on the Water dragon to the limit. He is wearing a breastplate with seashell designs on it, symbolic of the ever-present life force that allows humans to expose the body and mind to new and sometimes dangerous adventures, but protects the soul which is eternal. The water is full of other Water dragons, mermaids, and sea creatures. These creatures all symbolize the active seed-forms of manifestation that dwell within the sea-womb of the cauldron of creation. The Knight has a chalice fastened to his belt, and is reveling in his ride. The girl's face, seen behind him, represents his hidden feminine side. All humans possess both masculine and feminine energies within them, energies they must learn to balance for success in life.

Divinatory Meaning

Be prepared for an unexpected visit from someone you admire. Remember, a dreamer who is balanced between the dreams and reality accomplishes the most. You may have a pleasant outing with someone you care for deeply.

Queen of Cups

Strong psychic feelings.

Queen of Cups

The Queen of Cups is a regal, mature woman. She sits on her throne of shells with confidence in her abilities to rule the tides of emotions (the waves behind her), not be ruled by them. One arm is resting on the arm of the throne and holding a rich-looking chalice. She is very much aware that the cauldron of primordial energy will never run dry; that she will always have access to energy for magickal manifestation. The other hand rests on the arm of the throne, while a tiny Water dragon coils its tail around her wrist. This little companion and co-magician dragon will ever be close at hand to help the Queen in her magickal and spiritual work. The crown of pearls and shells on her head symbolizes her knowledge of how to reach the spiritual enlightenment found in the sacred center of her very being. Her throne of authority sits on the very edge of the sand where it meets the waters of the sea, a representation of her closeness to the Goddess.

Divinatory Meaning

This card indicates a feminine influence with a strong loving and protecting nature. This will be a time of quiet contentment with life. A period of strong psychic feelings makes you more aware of spiritual goals.

King of Cups

Emotional events.

King of Cups

A regal, older man stands before a throne made out of shell. He wears a crown with pearls on the spiky tips. In one hand he holds a chalice trimmed with scallop shells. His other hand lies on the head of a Water dragon that lies wrapped around the throne. The throne stands on a beach, strewn with shells, starfish, and driftwood. The King of Cups has moved to a state of being where he is no longer ruled by the tides of emotions. He has earned his throne, which represents security and stability in the midst of emotions (the water of the sea). His crown with its pearls symbolizes spiritual enlightenment found in the sacred center of every human, the discovery of which enabled him to escape the emotional extremes of life. The shells (continuing life from one cycle to another) and the starfish (pentacle of protection) have come from the sea, which is the cauldron of creation and rebirth. Through the King's companionship with the Water dragon he has learned how to use emotional energy in a more positive way.

Divinatory Meaning

This card represents a loving and caring masculine influence. There is a possibility of a journey across water. You may experience an episode of up and down emotions.

Ace of Pentacles

Material success.

Ace of Pentacles

Three baby dragons are hatching out of a nest set on a rocky cliff with a tangle of bare trees and roots about them. Representing the Earth Egg, or pool of physical possibilities, this card symbolizes the fledgling energies awakening to a new cycle of existence or experience. The events in life are bare as the trees at this point, but hold the unseen ability to burst forth in joy and happiness (leaves). The events in life (trees) are rooted in stability (rock), their roots running deep into the past of this lifetime, or even into past lives. A vine clings to the tree in the foreground, symbolizing fertility of thought, word, and deed. A five-point star is clearly engraved just below the ledge that holds the nest, representing the underlying protection that is always available if we will only become aware of its presence. In the distance is a rugged mountain, the gateway to the spiritual. From the beginning point in a new cycle or journey, it is difficult to determine how the mountain will be reached and what it will offer when we get there. The seeker must awaken from spiritual slumber and make an effort before the desired goal can be attained.

Divinatory Meaning

A prosperous cycle is now beginning. Material success is now within your grasp. With a little effort, this time could be the beginning of a profitable career.

Two of Pentacles

Harmony through changes.

Two of Pentacles

A young woman walks across a log over a canyon, balancing a tiny dragon in each hand. She is not afraid of failure, for she wears the pentacle of protection and has her attention concentrated on each step of the journey, not the deep canyon beneath her. Her faith in herself gives her the ability to safely cross this obstacle in her path. Each of the two dragons has a medallion with a five-point star of protection around its neck. The number two symbolizes the balance of opposites, as well as both Goddess and God. The dragons are her personal astral guides, powerful for their small size and filled with knowledge that will aid their friend. A larger Earth dragon watches behind her, ready to help if the need arises. Faces of dragons, animals, and humans are seen in the rocks of the canyon. Even though the canyon appears to be an obstacle or barrier, it is filled with watchful entities of the astral realms, entities who can form a strong foundation of fellowship and cooperation.

Divinatory Meaning

Prepare to juggle two life-events at once without losing control. You will know harmony and contentment even though there are changes going on around you. This is a time of ups and downs in moods and energy.

Three of Pentacles

Profitable skills; satisfaction.

Three of Pentacles

A man is painting a five-point star or pentacle on the door of his castle. Two other pentacles are already painted, thus bringing the number to three. Three is the number of the Goddess, but it also represents the feminine side of his nature. He has sought and cultivated this feminine nature, thus making himself a more complete person. He is happy with what he is doing, using the skills he studied to make his life more productive and joyful. By developing his positive talents, whatever they might be, the man is fulfilling the destiny of this life. His castle represents his present life; the door symbolizes the entrance to the Inner Mysteries of the spiritual path. By placing this entrance to the spiritual in a major place in his life, the man is successful in all his endeavors. By using his talents to mark this door, the man can easily enter any time he wishes. However, the pentacles he has placed there will keep out those who would try to destroy his endeavors because of jealousy or spite. Three little Earth dragons sit over the door watching him. These creatures are his astral companions and friends, his guides on his spiritual journeys.

Divinatory Meaning

Material gain and success could come through a craft, hobby, or creative endeavor. This is an excellent time to learn profitable skills. Satisfaction can be gained at the end of a project.

Four of Pentacles

Grasping at money.

Four of Pentacles

A woman is clutching four disks with pentacles on them, while a large dragon watches and opens its mouth in anger. Little dragons dart at her from their flight above her head. The woman has stolen the disks from the hoard on which the dragon sits. If she had been worthy and had worked toward her goal of obtaining the disks in a positive way, the dragon would have shared them gladly. The little dragons try to act as her conscience; by getting her attention, they hope to make her look at her negative actions. However, the woman is determined that what she wants should be hers, even if that possession belongs to another. Her subconscious will defeat her in the end, and she will lose all she thinks she has gained, for her hair (symbol of her personal power and fertile energies) is bound by a chain. In this life or the next, the karma she has created will take away her freedom of choice.

Divinatory Meaning

You or someone close to you is very money oriented. This card indicates a person who has an unhealthy grasping control of finances. You could receive gifts, even a possible inheritance.

Five of Pentacles

Loss; unpleasant differences.

Five of Pentacles

A man and a woman walk away from each other, each determined that their way or opinion is the only one. Five broken disks with pentacles lie on the ground between them. These disks symbolize the life, friendship, cooperation, and/or love built between them, now destroyed because of ego and lack of compromise. Five dragons in the sky above them scream their anger and displeasure. Little dragons hiss at each other over the broken disks. The balance of the spiritual forces they have cultivated with their relationship has been upset, turning positive energies and events into negative ones.

Divinatory Meaning

Take care or there may be a loss of home or job. Differences arise that could divide friends or lovers. There may be a period of deep loneliness.

Six of Pentacles

Just rewards.

Six of Pentacles

A large dragon holds out a claw filled with coins to an old man with a cane. Beside the dragon, a little girl in tattered clothing hugs the dragon. The unlimited forces of the Universe work on the constant balancing of positive and negative. All we need do is seek and ask for the help we need. The child represents the hidden seed of trust and confidence within each of us that leads to a new cycle, even though we may be in the midst of sorrow. The child is completely unafraid of universal forces, subconsciously understanding that trust brings help and answers to our problems. Six pentacles can be seen on the cobblestones, leading from the struggling man to the glowing dragon. Our paths are full of signposts, directing us away from the negative and to the positive, if only we will be observant.

Divinatory Meaning

You will be receiving what is due you, positive or negative. Someone repays a past loan of money or time. Revive your outlook on life by helping others who are in need.

Seven of Pentacles

Anxiety; progress stopped.

Seven of Pentacles

A large dragon lies sleeping in a cave, with seven small dragons sleeping around it. Seven pentacles are carved into the stones. Spirals of creation-destruction cover the sandy floor. The opening of the cave can be seen beyond the dragons, leading to the bright glow of sunlight. Although protection is available, the seeker has not awakened the powers of creation and manifestation within the individual spirit. Those powers are now dormant, their help inactive. Nothing moves within the cave, or the deeply hidden center of creativity. No effort has been made to establish a firm link with the spiritual realms.

Divinatory Meaning

Progress could be stopped in the middle of a project. Be careful or you may be involved in bad investments. There is a possibility of anxiety about finances. Your effort is spent on the wrong things.

Eight of Pentacles

New skills; new opportunities.

Eight of Pentacles

A large teaching dragon sits with an ancient book of wisdom in its claws. It is reading to the young boy and girl who sit before it. Eight tiny dragons sit around the children and on their shoulders. They all sit in a beautiful garden with a fountain just beyond them. The large dragon represents the main astral teacher and guide who tries to guide each person into a positive path of life. The fountain of renewal rises in the midst of the garden, symbolic of the orderly conscious mind. However, the fountain is connected with the subconscious mind and the emotions, thus showing that correct use of water (emotions) has a regenerating effect on the garden (conscious mind). The circular wall that surrounds the fountain is a birth symbol. Birth of any idea or goal originates in the subconscious mind and the emotions, then makes its appearance in the conscious mind and reality. The smaller dragons are the helpful astral entities and companions.

Divinatory Meaning

Take the time to learn new skills. Use your knowledge to create new opportunities. Karma brings good things your way; you will reap the benefits of past work.

Nine of Pentacles

Comfortable aloneness.

Nine of Pentacles

A dragon and a man sit along the edge of a forest. It is a sunny day, and many small animals and birds are around the dragon and the man. The man is at one with Nature and his astral teacher, the dragon. The birds are messages from spirit, sent to help him make decisions and find his path in life. The wolves in the background represent the strength, cunning, and wisdom he is learning, while the squirrel of resourcefulness, the rabbit of fertility, and the little mice of self-preservation help him to create a balanced attitude toward life.

Divinatory Meaning

You feel comfortable, safe, and at ease with yourself. There will soon be a pleasant period of being alone. A journey into Nature can renew your outlook on life and recharge your energies.

Ten of Pentacles

Property; business.

Ten of Pentacles

A man and a woman stand on the bridge of a castle before the open gate. They have worked hard and earned the right to cross the bridge between the conscious and subconscious minds, or travel freely in the astral realms. This bridge also symbolizes their rewards in the physical life for their work toward a balanced life. By their feet are three cats, representing the independence, resourcefulness, and healing they have learned. The dragon on the wall above them oversees their protection on all astral journeys as well as in their physical life. The tiny dragons flying around them are their astral companions. Above the arch of the open door are ten pentacles; ten is often considered to be a completion number, an ending that heralds a new beginning.

Divinatory Meaning

This is a good period to acquire a house or property. If you have been considering starting a business, this could foretell a period of success. A pleasant family gathering renews your confidence and happiness.

Page of Pentacles

News of money.

Page of Pentacles

The Page of Pentacles is shown as a young boy standing beside his Guardian dragon. A medallion with a pentacle of protection hangs about the boy's neck, while the dragon holds a similar pentacle between its front claws. The boy is completely at ease and trusts his astral companion to take him where he needs to go and show him what he needs to see. The boy rests one hand on the dragon while the other holds an ancient book; its title is *The Meaning of Dreams*. Above his head are misty images of dream-like dragons. This book symbolizes the knowledge available in the subconscious mind, knowledge that can be accessed if one is willing to learn how. This mystical knowledge often presents itself in the form of dreams, as represented by the misty dragons above the boy's head. Dreams are frequently presented to the dreamer in symbolic form. Without a conscious study of mystical symbols and their personal meaning to the dreamer, the dreams cannot be correctly interpreted and understood. On the floor, a tiny dragon and a cat touch noses, showing that similar ideas often come in different forms.

Divinatory Meaning

News of money comes unexpectedly. You could experience a period of prophetic dreams. Now is the opportunity to delve into a new area of study and knowledge.

Knight of Pentacles

Gains and losses.

Knight of Pentacles

A teenage girl, clad in a golden breastplate and helmet, stands beside a large dragon on a rocky hill. They are watching men building a stone house below. The girl has a Celtic sword slung at her belt; beside the sword is a bag with a pentacle on the side. From her vantage point at the gates to the spiritual realm, the girl can clearly see the labor that goes into each life; this labor creates a personal space for the individual, a necessity for the maintenance of individuality and personal identity. The stones of the hillside symbolize primordial power; this symbolism is repeated in the stones used to build the house. There is an unlimited supply of creative, primordial energy upon which any person may draw to manifest what is needed in life, if they are willing to put forth the effort. The sword and the bag with the pentacle represent the spiritual strength for defense.

Divinatory Meaning

There could be a gain or loss in finances. Salary increase is possible. The chance to purchase real estate may come about. A loan is repaid.

Queen of Pentacles

Future plans.

Queen of Pentacles

The Queen of Pentacles is represented by an older woman dressed in rich earth-tone robes. She wears a crown with a pentacle centered on her forehead. Her dragon-throne is carved of stone. She has earned the right to sit on the mighty throne through her diligent study and compassion for all creatures on the Earth. On the back of the throne, just above her head, is carved a large dragon, symbolic of her constant contact with the astral and spiritual realms. Just above her head is a shining pentacle of power and protection. In one hand she holds a wand with a golden star at its tip. A mistress of psychic power, the woman knows how to manifest her desires, yet she does this with great control and consideration. The other hand rests on the head of a dragon lying beside the throne, her astral companion. The red of her cloak symbolizes the blood of life, while the brown of her gown reveals her connections with Earth and the powers of Nature. Her white undergown reveals the closeness she has established with spiritual realms. By her side is a small ornate table holding a candle and a crystal ball, while books are scattered at her feet. Through knowledge and study (the books), this woman has learned to see clearly (candle) into the past and future (the crystal ball).

Divinatory Meaning

This card indicates a feminine influence who is good with finances, but critical and demanding. An opportunity will come to reap good benefits after a long time of labor. This is an auspicious time for making future plans.

King of Pentacles

Success in business and money.

King of Pentacles

The King of Pentacles is portrayed here as a regal, older man standing beside a richly decorated and carved wooden throne in a forest. Vine-covered boughs make a canopy over the throne. A large dragon lies near the man's feet. The man's right hand rests on a sword with a pentacle at its pommel. The other hand rests on the back of the throne. He wears a crown with dark green stones in it. Over the seat of the throne is thrown a green cloak with Celtic symbols on it. Through years of experience and spiritual study, this man has earned the reward and responsibility of being a master of Earth energies. His throne (stability and balance in life) is one with Nature. This symbolism is intensified with the carvings of pentacles (protection), spirals (creative-destructive energy), and dragon teeth (spiritual protection) on the throne. The vine of life (the feminine and creative side of each human) binds the physical manifestation of life with all of Nature. Even the green robe with its mystical symbols shows the continued connection in all of the man's life. Confident in the path to knowledge that he has chosen, the King proudly displays the Celtic Tree of Life on his vest and the pentacle of protection on his sword of justice.

Divinatory Meaning

This card represents a masculine influence that can be domineering, yet wise and reliable. You may have business with a banker or the head of a business. Success in money matters is now possible. Beware of stubbornness that could alienate others.

Chapter 5

Tarot Layouts

For those who are new at reading tarot cards, there are a few basic procedures and actions to keep in mind. Have a clear question (and only one question at a time) in mind while you shuffle the cards. Shuffle the deck until it feels right to you. Then cut the cards into three piles and put them back together in a different order than you cut them. Traditionally, the cards were cut with the left hand. Do not begin reading the cards until you have them all laid out in the chosen pattern.

At times you may find it difficult to read for yourself, especially if you feel very strongly about the question asked. It is possible for some people to influence the cards through their strong feelings and psychic powers. If this is the case, you might want to exchange readings with another tarot reader.

The Expanded Celtic Cross

Some variation of this tarot layout is common and well known to most users of tarot cards. I prefer to have the extra cards in the layout as I feel they help to clarify certain points. If the outcome is muddled or unclear, you can lay out two more cards on the end (cards 12 and 13). However, if this still does not help, you need to rephrase the question. Perhaps you actually have two or more other questions in mind instead of concentrating on just one question.

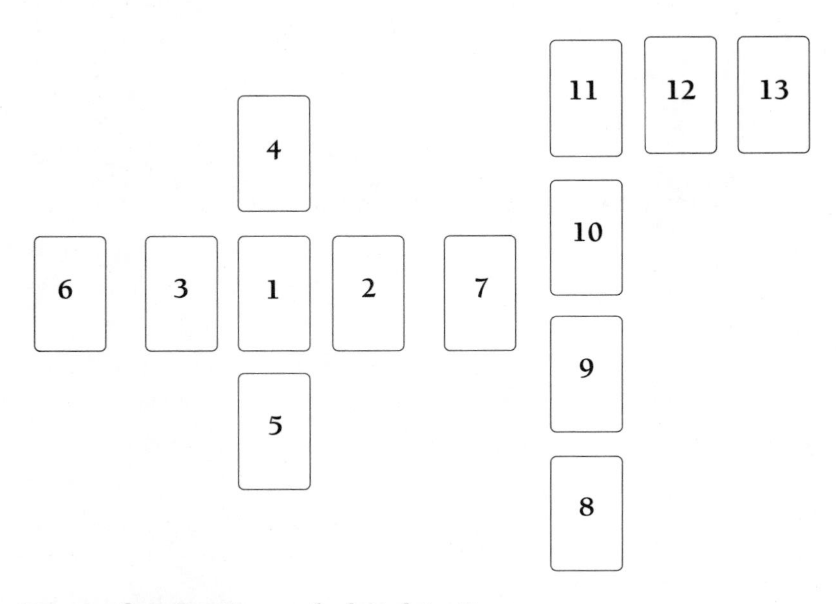

Layout for the Expanded Celtic Cross

1: This card represents the inquirer.
2: Helpful forces around the inquirer.
3: Opposing forces around the inquirer.
4: Present happenings or frame of mind.
5: Subconscious feelings of the inquirer.
6: Past influences on the question.
7: Possible immediate future.
8: Fears and attitudes of the inquirer.
9: Influence and opinions of family and friends.
10: Results of actions and thoughts of the inquirer.
11: Final outcome at the present time.
12: Extra card for further clarification of card 11.
13: Extra card for further clarification of card 11.

Influence of the Elements

This layout may be used to answer any question or to clarify weak areas in your life that may be contributing to problems. By reading each card position in relation to one of the Elements, you can also identify, understand, and correct any potential imbalances that could affect your immediate future.

Lay the cards out in their numerical order, beginning in the center with Spirit. Although we speak of there being only four Elements, there is an esoteric fifth one: Spirit, or that affecting your spiritual being and soul.

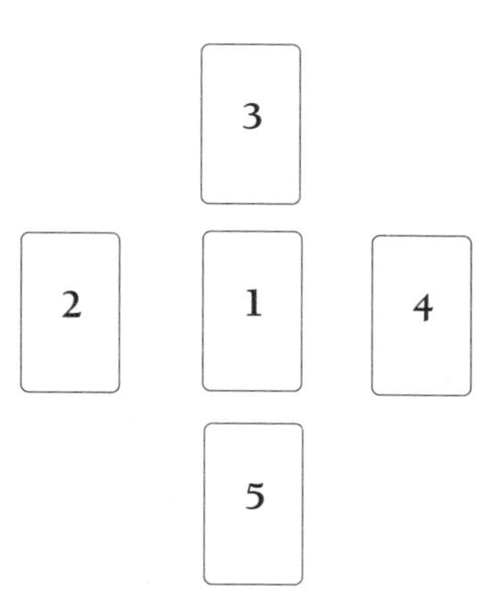

Layout for the Influence of the Elements

1: Spirit—the spiritual health of your life.
2: Air (East)—the mental part of your life.
3: Fire (South)—your energy or the movement of events.
4. Water (West)—your emotional state.
5: Earth (North)—your physical self.

Past Life, Present Influence

Many times the problems with which we wrestle in this life have their roots in other lives. When you have done all you can to make things better and it has not worked well or at all, you need to go further back in your personal history and find the cause. This is usually referred to as karma, a term which has unfortunately come to be used only in its negative connotation. Actually, karma is both positive and negative. We not only build up negative karma, which we must put right or pay for at some time, but we also build up a store of positive karma that can benefit us.

Although this layout will not tell you in detail what life and where you built the karma now affecting you, it will help in understanding the basics behind the present problems.

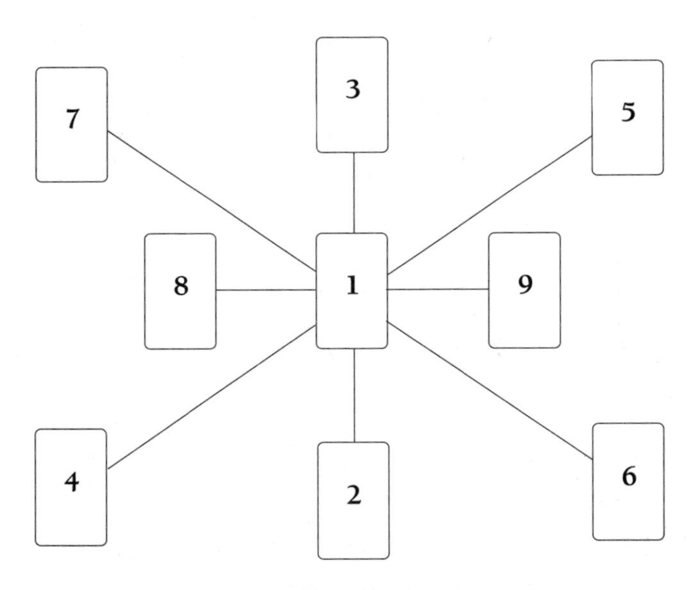

Layout for Past Life, Present Influence

1: Present face the inquirer shows to the world.
2: Past physical state affecting the question.
3: Present physical state.
4: Past mental state affecting the question.
5: Present mental state.
6: Past spiritual state affecting the question.
7: Present spiritual state.
8: Past emotional state affecting the question.
9: Present emotional state.

This layout requires much introspection. You are comparing traits and/or conditions from your past lives to your present life, in an effort to find stumbling blocks. Past life conditions continue to influence our present subconscious mind, often causing us to act or react in ways which seem out of character. For example, if card 4 were the Seven of Swords and card 5 were the Two of Cups, you may subconsciously destroy close relationships or friendships by striving for control over the other person. Card 4 reveals a past life trait of ruthlessly dominating others in relationships, a trait that may be sabotaging your present life desire for a close, meaningful companionship. By being aware of this subconscious influence from the past, you can learn to stop this destructive habit pattern.

Path to a Goal

This layout only works on a question about a specific goal you are trying to reach or gain in your life. If you do not have a clear goal in mind, the reading will be confused. This is an excellent method for determining if you should change certain patterns so you can reach your goal or if continuing on the same path will work. It may point out to you that this goal is not the right one for you. Card 11, the outcome, will tell you what will happen if you keep doing the things you are doing now.

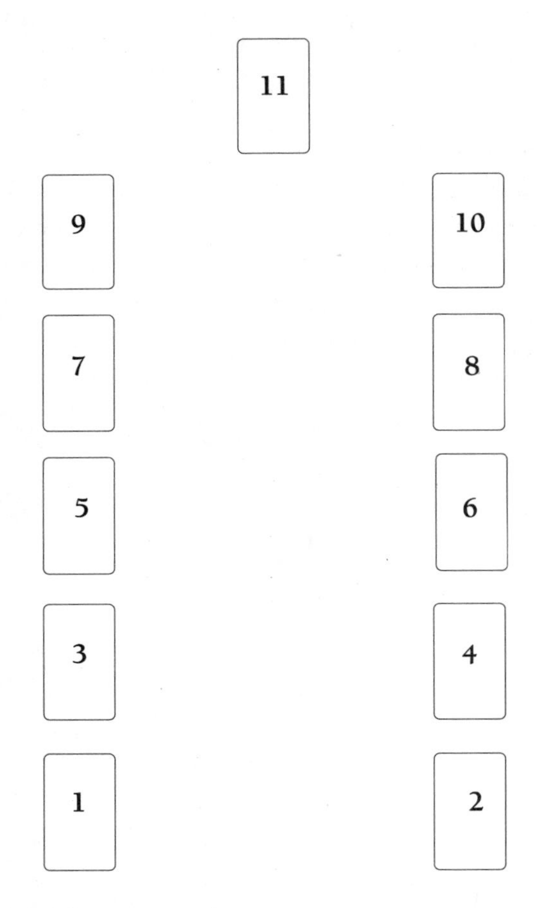

Layout for Path to a Goal

1: Health; physical and emotional.
2: Health; physical and emotional.
3: Mental attitude.
4: Mental attitude.
5: Relationships.
6: Relationships.
7: Career.
8: Career.
9: Spiritual path.
10: Spiritual path.
11: Outcome of the present path.

Everyone has a visible life path that you show to the world, and a hidden life path that represents your deepest conditioning and desires. The left column of cards represents the hidden life path, the "secret" you that few people ever know, while the right column represents the visible life path, the "exposed" face that you reveal to the public. A harmonious life will have these two life paths primarily balanced with little opposition between them. For example, if card 3 were The Hanged Man and card 4 the Eight of Pentacles, your hidden self avoids making decisions, rather than be wrong, while your visible side wants to learn new skills and take advantage of sudden opportunities. Depending upon the balance and strength of the other cards in the layout, this may result in taking too long to make up your mind about opportunities, and you find them slipping through your fingers time after time.

Chapter 6

Dragon Tarot Candle Spells

Candle-burning magick has been used for centuries. The technique is simple, requires few tools, and can be done by even the newest student in magick. You will need a space where you can safely leave candles to burn completely out without being disturbed, several nonflammable candleholders, a supply of various colored candles, and your deck of *Celtic Dragon Tarot* cards. The candles can be either the six-inch straights or votives. You can burn a magenta candle with any of the following spells to bring about the results quicker.

If you like incense, you can burn sticks or cones of frankincense, sandalwood, or lotus as general, all-purpose scents. To add an extra touch of magickal power, you can also set certain stones either on or near the cards. A list of candle color meanings and stone powers can be found in the appendices.

Begin your chosen spell by putting the appropriate colored candle or candles in the fire-proof holders. Set the listed cards in the arrangement given. Light the incense and put out your stones, if you plan to use these. Speak the Opening Chant (see page 180). Light the candles and say the special verse for the particular spell. Concentrate a few moments on the tarot cards and your objective. When you are finished, speak the Closing Chant (also on page 180). Leave the candles in a safe place to burn completely out. This may take several hours.

Caution: *If you feel ill at ease leaving the candle to burn out on a table or altar, you could place it in a sink or bathtub for added safety.* Dispose of the cold wax and put away the cards and stones.

Opening Chant

I move outside the limits of time to work my spell.
The dragons help me weave the universal energy.
The things that now exist become what I desire.
The tides of magick answer unto me.

Closing Chant

My thanks to the dragons, great and small,
Who came in answer to my call.
We wove the magick, wild and free,
And as I will, so shall it be.

Getting Things Moving

Cards needed: The World, Eight of Wands, and Six of Wands.

Candles: white, magenta, and violet.

Set the candles out in a line on your altar, with the white in the middle, the magenta on the left, and the violet on the right. Place The World card behind the white candle, the Eight of Wands behind the magenta, and the Six of Wands behind the violet.

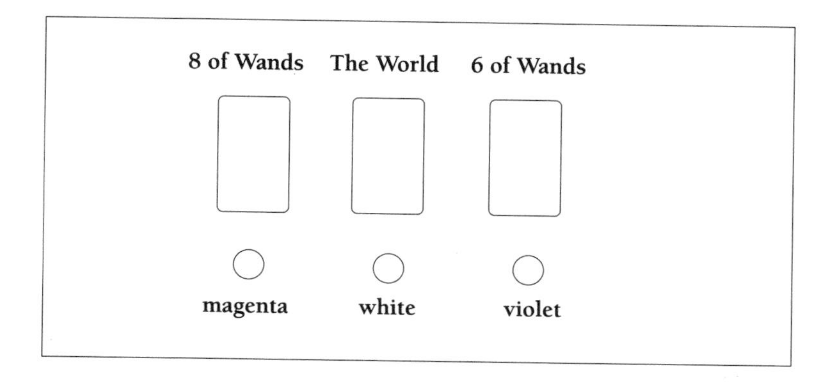

Say:

> ***All barriers are removed. All hindrances are gone.***
> ***The stagnant areas of my life move forward***
> ***to provide me with the needed opportunities.***
> ***Nothing and no one can stop my progress.***

Blessing and/or Healing of Pets

Cards needed: Nine of Cups and The Star.

Candles: brown and blue.

Set the two candles side by side on the altar. Place the Nine of Cups card behind the brown candle and The Star behind the blue.

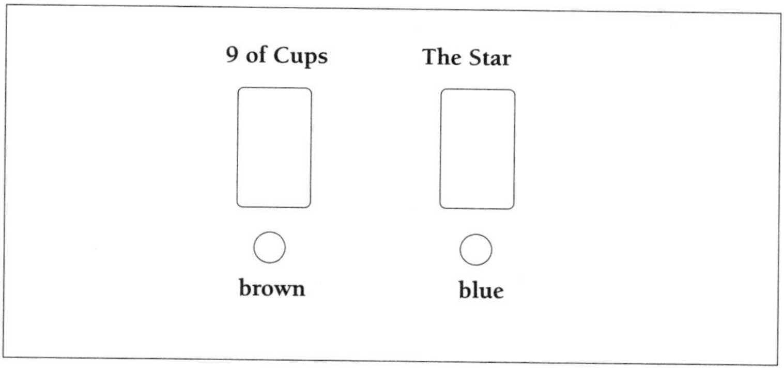

9 of Cups
The Star
brown
blue

Say:

> ***All you dragons of Earth and healing, all you Earth elementals and lovers of animals, bless and heal (pet's name). Give her (him) good health and happiness once more. Weave my love for (pet's name) into your magick, for love is the greatest healer of all.***

Gaining Creativity

Cards needed: Temperance, Ace of Cups, and Three of Pentacles.

Candle: yellow.

Set the candle in the center of your altar with one card on each side of it and one behind it.

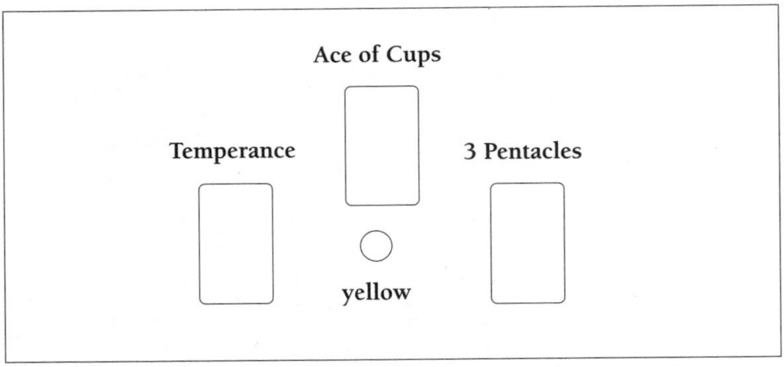

Ace of Cups

Temperance **3 Pentacles**

yellow

Say:

> ***I reach out to the universal well of ideas and inspiration. My mind is open to receive what I need. Creativity flows freely into my thoughts.***

Healing

Cards needed: The Star, Three of Cups, and Ace of Cups.

Candles: white, blue, and red.

Set the white candle in the center of your altar, with the blue on the left and the red on the right. Place The Star card behind the white, the Three of Cups behind the blue, and the Ace of Cups behind the red.

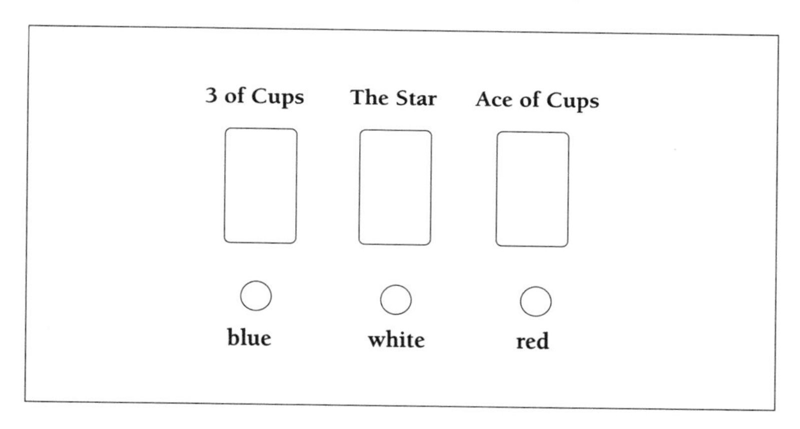

Say:

> ***All vibrations that cause the illness of (person's name) are driven away. Healing energies flow into her (his) body, mind, and spirit. Balance of health is restored. She (he) is healthy, happy, and whole once more.***

Change of Luck

Cards needed: The Wheel, The World, and Six of Cups.

Candles: orange, yellow, indigo, and black.

Set the orange and yellow candles in a vertical line in the center of your altar. Put the indigo candle on the left of these, the black on the right. Place the cards above the candles in the order they are listed.

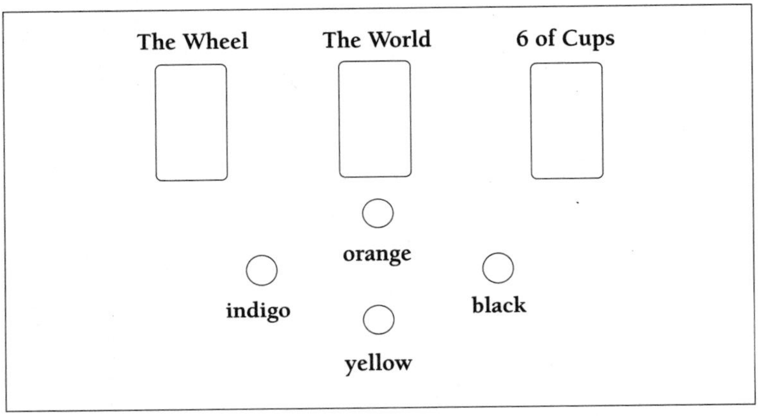

The Wheel **The World** **6 of Cups**

orange

indigo **black**

yellow

Say:

> ***The Wheel of Fate begins to turn and changes my luck. All negative thoughts and deeds against me are barred from affecting my life. New opportunities and paths open before me. I am surrounded by positive vibrations.***

Developing the Psychic

Cards needed: High Priestess, The Star, Queen of Cups, and Page of Pentacles.

Candles: silver, gold, brown, and purple.

Place the silver and gold candles in a vertical line in the center of your altar with the brown on the left and the purple on the right. Arrange the cards above the candles in the order they are listed.

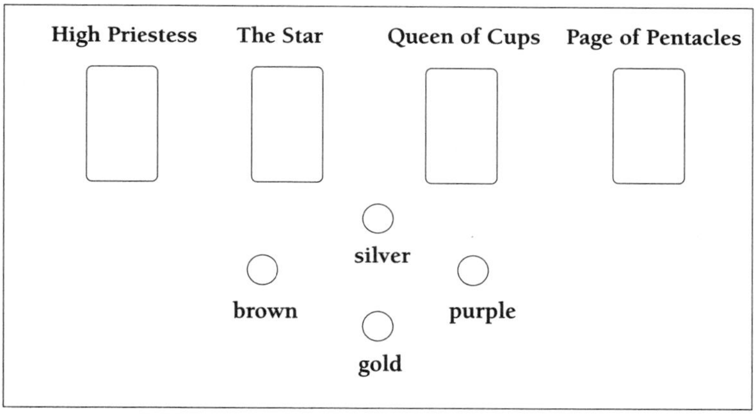

High Priestess **The Star** **Queen of Cups** **Page of Pentacles**

silver

brown **purple**

gold

Say:

> ***I open myself to positive guidance in developing my psychic abilities. I will do all I can to study and learn. I trust in the Goddess (God) to send the right spiritual teachers to help me. I will use my talents to aid both myself and others who are in need of guidance and direction.***

To Gain Guiding Dreams

Cards needed: Page of Pentacles, The Moon.

Candle: silver.

Put the candle in the center of your altar with the two cards above it.

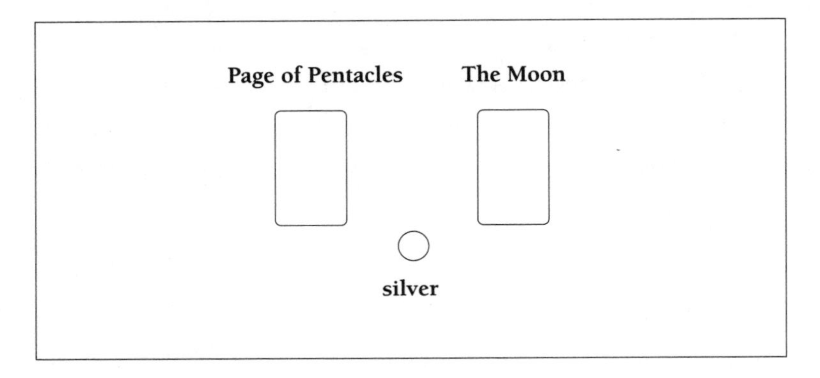

Say:

> ***Dragons of light and inspiration, dragons of the spiritual realms, send to me dreams of guidance and knowledge. I need guidance on (state the reason you want guiding dreams). I cannot see what is truth and what is illusion. The path I should take is veiled in mist. Come to me in my dreams, and show me the right way to go.***

Protection

Cards needed: Strength, Seven of Wands, The Chariot, and Four of Swords.

Candles: black, gray, indigo, and purple.

Set the candles in a line in the order listed. Place the Strength card above the black candle, the Seven of Wands above the gray, The Chariot above the indigo, and the Four of Swords above the purple. If you desire, you can place a picture of yourself alone, or with your family and/or pets, on the altar also.

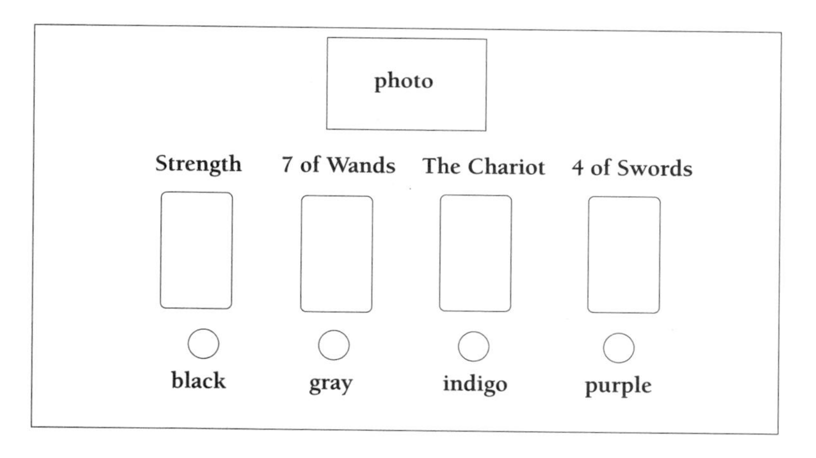

Say:

> ***Black binds all harm and keeps it far away. Gray hides me in a safe cloud of illusion. Indigo dissolves all magick against me and stops all gossip and lies. Purple breaks bad luck and drives away evil. No one with evil intent or thought can cross this barrier set by the dragons.***

Finding True Love

Cards needed: Nine of Cups, Four of Wands, and Two of Cups.

Candles: pink, green, and blue.

Set the pink candle in the middle of your altar. Place the green candle to the left and a little below it. Put the blue candle to the right and a little below it. Lay the Nine of Cups above the pink candle, the Four of Wands by the green one, and the Two of Cups by the blue one.

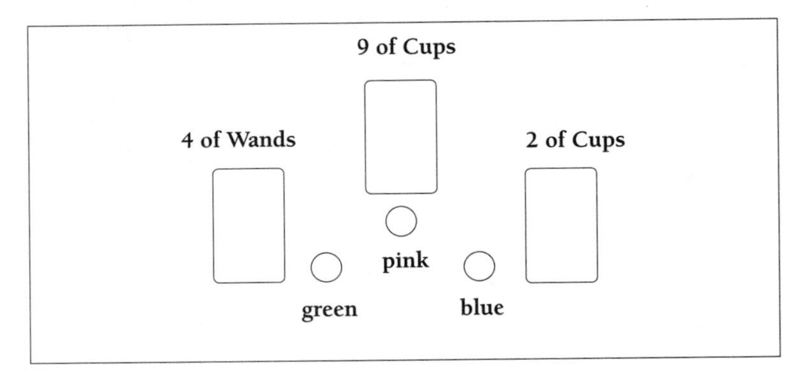

Say:

> ***I open my heart and arms to the true love meant for me. I am beautiful in spirit, thus drawing to me another with a beautiful spirit. Happiness will fill my heart and life. Great dragons, bring to me a true and lasting love.***

Gaining a Good Job or Bettering Your Career

Cards needed: The Chariot, The Sun, Three of Wands, and Page of Wands.

Candles: orange, gold, brown, and yellow.

Place the orange candle in the center of your altar, with the gold above it, the brown on the left, and the yellow on the right. Put The Chariot and The Sun cards above the gold candle, the Three of Wands beside the left candle, and the Page of Wands beside the right one.

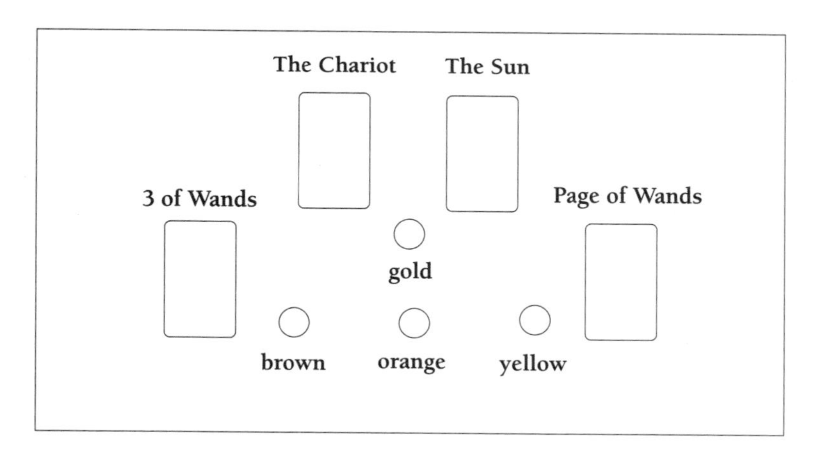

Say:

> *Open the doors that will help me to gain a good job (further my career). Aid me in listening to the voices of spiritual wisdom, the voices that will guide me in making the right decisions. Give me the right words and the appropriate actions that will turn the tide and make me successful.*

Help in Legal Matters

Cards needed: Justice, The World, and Nine of Cups.

Candles: gray, orange, indigo, purple, black, and gold.

Set the candles in a line on your altar in the order given. Place the cards above the candles, in the order they are listed.

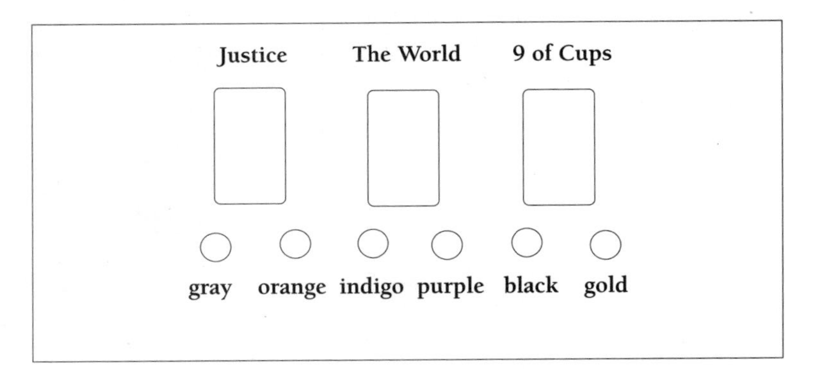

Say:

> ***Gray mists to hide what I must do. Orange light to change my luck and give me power. Indigo strength to stop gossip and lies. Purple power to break bad luck and drive away evil. Great black walls to protect me from my enemies. Sun-gold beams to give me good fortune and success. I stand surrounded by these powerful lights. I ask the dragon's help to succeed in my case.***

Gaining Prosperity

Cards needed: Ten of Pentacles, The Empress, and Ace of Pentacles.

Candles: gold and green.

Place the candles in the center of your altar. Put the cards above the candles, in the order they are given.

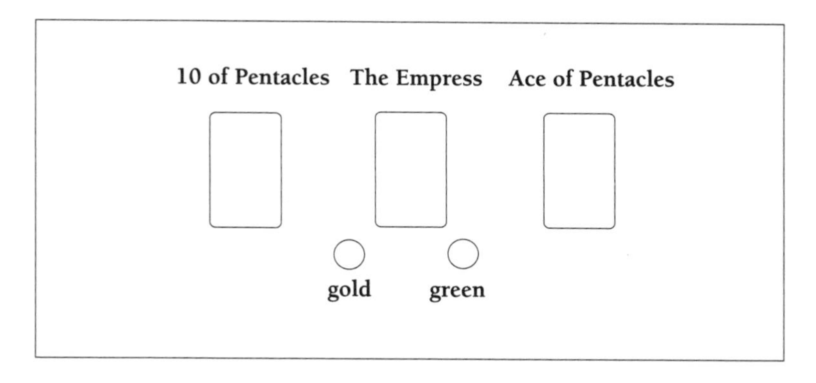

Say three times:

> *Good vibrations, prosperity, success and money,*
> *come to me. All good things grow, no fear or strife,*
> *prosperity comes into my life.*

Removal of Obstacles

Cards needed: Strength, The World, and Five of Wands (covered).

Candles: black and white.

Put the candles in the center of your altar. Place the Strength, the Five of Wands, and The World cards above the candles, with the Five of Wands covered by The World card.

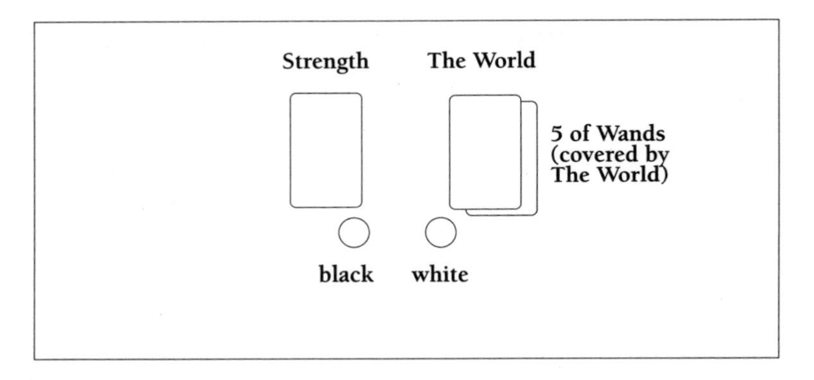

Say:

> ***Great dragons of great fire and power, help me in this needful hour. Remove the walls that block my way. Reveal the gate to a whole new way to walk a path of happiness great. Let all freedom to move be my fate.***

Making a Decision

Cards needed: Judgment, The Magician, Two of Wands, and Eight of Pentacles.

Candles: purple and silver.

Place the purple and silver candles side by side in the center of your altar. Arrange the Judgment and The Magician cards above the candles. Put the Two of Wands on the left of the candles and the Eight of Pentacles on the right.

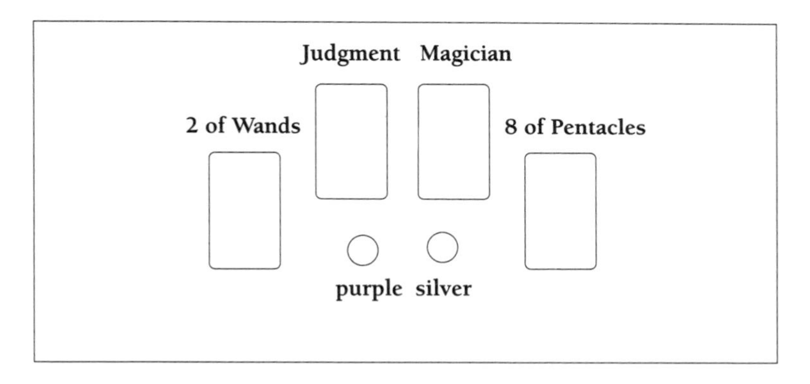

Say:

> ***Great dragons of wisdom, I must make a decision about (state the problem). I cannot clearly see the right choice. Grant me the wisdom and correct information that will aid me in deciding this problem. Send me the message in words or dreams or actions. Guide my steps onto the right path for me.***

New Beginnings

Cards needed: The Fool, Death, Ace of Wands, and The World.

Candles: yellow and red.

Place the candles side by side in the center of your altar. Put the cards in a line above them, in the order given.

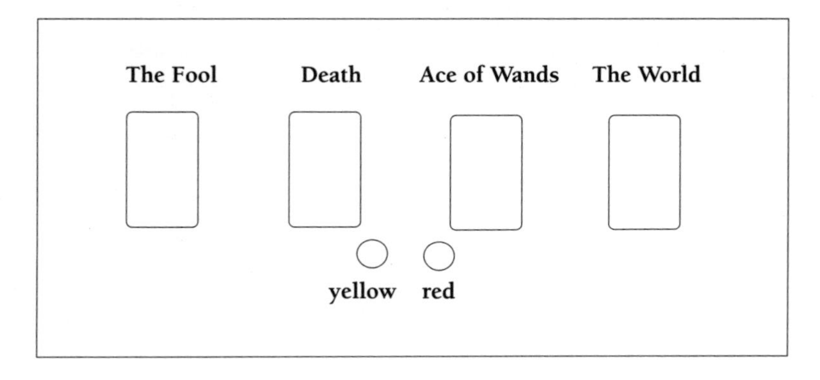

Say:

> ***As the Fool and Dreamer follow the spiritual guiding voice within, so do I as I stand at a crossroads of life. This is my time of transformation and new beginnings. Make clear the proper path and guide me as I fearlessly walk down it. Guide me to all positive things that will make my world a joyous, happy, fruitful place to be.***

Chapter 7

Meditations

Meditation is a valuable tool, both for those in magick and for those who simply want to relieve stress or have wonderful astral experiences. This spiritual practice is not difficult once you discipline yourself to sit still for a short period of time. Following are simple instructions on how to relax into meditation, as well as short, guided meditations that will help you to explore the powers of dragon energy and interact with these wonderful creatures.

To a dedicated magician, or a person seeking spiritual paths, the path into other planes of existence is well worn; she/he never feels they have learned all there is to know. The magician follows the Otherworld path confident that she/he is not the first to do so, nor will she/he be the last. Such a person is driven by an inner yearning for growth on all levels of her/his being.

The experiences gained during meditation can help you make changes in your life, pick up your spirits when you are down, and provide you with new insights and goals. Rarely does the meditating person come out of the experience with nothing. The more you put into meditation, in terms of energy, discipline, and time, the more you will get in return.

If you are new to meditation, or concerned that thinking about where you want to go will hinder you, read the meditation into a tape recorder beforehand. Speak at a reasonable pace, not too fast or too slow; leave a silent period in the proper place so you can explore personally. It is also helpful if you record the preliminary relaxation technique at the beginning of the tape and follow it with the guided meditation itself. Be sure to include the part where you get rid of things that are bothering you. You do not want to carry these negative vibrations into meditation.

To meditate, sit in a comfortable chair in a place where you will not be disturbed. Silence the telephone, as its ringing is quite a jolt when you are deep in meditation. Soft instrumental music will help to mask small noises that might bother you. If you choose to burn incense, be certain that it will not drift toward you or become too thick in the room.

It is also helpful if you choose a card from the Celtic Dragon Tarot to study before the meditation. Examples of cards to use are listed before each meditation. Study these cards and think about their symbolism before you go into meditation. They will help your subconscious mind bring up the meditational happenings that will help you.

Relaxation Techniques

Begin each meditation by relaxing your body. Begin at your feet and end at the head. Mentally tell each part of your body to relax. Do not dwell on whether or not it is doing this, but just assume it is and move on. As you relax your body, you will find that your consciousness moves upward along with the relaxation. Spend extra time on your shoulders, neck, and throat, as these will be the most tense. As you relax your scalp, your consciousness will automatically move to an area just above your head. At this point you are ready to astral travel. Any time you desire to leave the meditation, all you have to do is think of your physical body and you will instantly return. You are never locked into a meditation.

The first thing you must always do is visualize or "sense" yourself surrounded by brilliant white light. Slowly breathe it in. This light will move with you during meditation and act as a protective spiritual barrier.

Then you need to see yourself standing on a bridge over a pond or river. Take all the negative events and people who are causing you trouble and throw them into the water. This act ensures that you do not clutter yourself with negative emotions.

These steps are necessary to having a positive and rewarding meditation, so be certain you include them in any meditation that you do.

Meeting Your Special Dragon

Cards needed for study: the Ace of Wands, Ace of Swords, Ace of Cups, and Ace of Pentacles.

Begin with your relaxation techniques. When finished, visualize yourself surrounded by white light. Then drop all your problems into the pond or river.

You find yourself on a mountaintop. Beyond you, in the distance, you see a volcano with smoke and steam floating from its crater. You turn to look behind and below you. Vast forests sparkle with bright blue lakes and twisting rivers. On the horizon you can see the twinkling edges of an ocean. The tan and ocher hues of distant sand dunes are a streak of color between the aquamarine ocean waters and the deep green of evergreen trees. You look up at the sky and see that storm clouds are rolling in over the mountains, although long shafts of brilliant sunlight break through the clouds to light up the hills and forests.

Suddenly, you are aware of various kinds of dragons in the scenery around you. The dark Chaos dragons roll and turn in the storm clouds, while the dragons of Light fly up and down the paths of sunlight. Earth dragons crawl beneath the thick canopy of tree branches. Fire dragons of all sizes play in the steam and heat of the volcano. Every lake and river is home to Water dragons, as is the distant ocean. Dragons of the desert and arid places haunt the hot dunes. You can feel the separate energy and power of each dragon as they call to you.

Hold out your hands and mentally call to the dragon to which you are attracted. Instantly, you are beside that dragon. You walk unharmed and unafraid in the dragon's domain. The dragon speaks to you, telling you things you need to know about improving your life on all levels.

When you are finished, you can return to your body, or you can return to the mountaintop and visit with another dragon. At any time that you feel uncomfortable with a particular dragon, you can end the visit. When you wish to end the meditation, simply think of your physical body.

When you are once more in your physical body, take several deep breaths to ground yourself. Open your eyes. You are once more entirely in the physical realm.

The Dragon of Changes

Cards needed for study: The Wheel, The Magician, and The Empress.

Begin with your relaxation techniques. When finished, visualize yourself surrounded by white light. Then drop all your problems into the pond or river.

You are standing at the edge of a wide lake. The sun is setting, turning the sky to beautiful shades of red and yellow and purple. The lake water laps gently at your feet. The shoreline is thick with cattails and rushes. Birds sing in the trees behind you. Dragonflies dart over the water, their wings flashing with brilliant colors. You notice that the lake water turns a much deeper blue at the center where it becomes very deep.

As you stand there, listening and watching the things about you, a bubbling begins in the lake and moves toward the shore where you are. A great Water dragon rises out of the lake. Its shiny scales gleam with a silvery blue color. The great eyes are golden and full of wisdom. Around its neck is a thick silver chain.

"Do you seek me for help in making changes?" the dragon asks.

When you answer "yes," the dragon holds out one paw and helps you get onto its great back.

"I will protect you with my magick," the dragon tells you. "You will breathe underwater as easily as you breathe in the air."

You hold onto the silver chain as the dragon dives deep into the waters of the lake. You are not afraid. You look at the fish swimming by, the water plants waving in the wake of the dragon's passage. Soon you see a great underwater castle ahead.

The dragon swims into the castle, and you discover that the water ends at the great doors. You get down and follow, as the dragon leads you off into a wide, long corridor. Soon you come to a large mirror hung on the stone wall.

"Show me a single thing you want changed," the dragon says. As you look into the mirror, you see there something in your life that you wish changed. See this event or problem as it really is at this time.

"Now you and I will use our magickal powers to create changes." The dragon takes your hand and together you turn the event or problem into a more positive energy pattern. If the event or problem does not completely change, ask the dragon what you must do to help make it turn into something different. Listen closely to what the dragon tells you.

If you have other needed changes, go down the corridor to the next mirror and repeat the magickal rite.

When you are finished, you may talk with the dragon for a time before it returns you to the shoreline.

At any time that you feel uncomfortable, you can end the visit. When you wish to end the meditation, simply think of your physical body.

When you are once more in your physical body, take several deep breaths to ground yourself. Open your eyes. You are once more entirely in the physical realm.

Riding the Dragon

Cards needed for study: the Knight of Wands, the Knight of Swords, the Knight of Cups, and the Knight of Pentacles.

Begin with your relaxation techniques. When finished, visualize yourself surrounded by white light. Then drop all your problems into the pond or river.

Close your eyes and visualize yourself astride the back of a great, dark dragon. The dragon is swiftly winging through the night, blowing great billows of smoke and fire. You feel the air rushing past and feel no fear at your experience. The dragon will never allow any harm to come to you.

The dragon asks you to name the problems in your life, the events that are causing you mental stress or emotional pain. You talk to the dragon about all of these. Remember, do not specifically intend harm to any person. Removing or diminishing the negative events will take care of any troublesome people without naming them.

The dragon asks if you want these problems eliminated. If you answer no, the dragon will return you to your physical body or take you on a sightseeing ride through beautiful places. If you answer yes, the dragon will dive down on the

problems, scattering them, turning them into ashes. Feel the excitement and rush of joy as you realize you are now free.

When the dragon is finished, you can talk with him/her further or you can return to your physical body and end the meditation.

When you are once more in your physical body, take several deep breaths to ground yourself. Open your eyes. You are once more entirely in the physical realm. Feel within yourself the power of the dragon. Know that you are going to win over all obstacles.

Spiritual Dragon Initiation

Cards needed for study: High Priestess and High Priest.

Begin with your relaxation techniques. When finished, visualize yourself surrounded by white light. Then drop all your problems into the pond or river.

Visualize yourself standing on a great rocky ledge. Before you is the mouth of a huge cave. It is shaped like the mouth of a dragon. Inside, from some deep, terrestrial fire, comes a red glow. You know you will not be harmed whatever you see or whatever happens. You are unafraid.

Enter the cave and follow the dim passageway deep into the Earth. After many twists and turns, you enter a circular, subterranean chamber with crystals embedded in the walls. There are stone benches along the walls.

At the four cardinal points of this circular chamber you see deep pits or cracks in the rocky floor. From these cracks comes the red glow of fire from deep under the Earth. It lights the chamber and reflects in rainbow flashes off the crystals. Sometimes you see the shadowy forms of dragons around the dim edges of the chamber.

In the center of this chamber of light and shadow stands a gem-encrusted altar. On the altar is a jeweled chalice.

A deep, Otherworld voice of a dragon comes to you from across the chamber. "Are you here for initiation?"

You answer "yes," and walk forward to stand before the altar as the dragons move closer to surround you. You see their glowing eyes and flashes of light that reflects off their great scales. You can hear the sound of their leathery wings and sharp claws on the rocky floor, but you are not afraid.

"By what name are you known in our realm?" one of them asks.

You must answer with your magickal name. You feel the power sent to you from all sides by the half-seen dragons. Listen for any messages that they may give you.

Finally, you hear the deep voice of a dragon saying, "Drink from the chalice."

You lift the heavy jeweled cup and drink the contents. You can feel the dragon magick coursing through your body, seeping into your bones. You set the chalice back on the altar.

You go to sit on one of the benches and talk with the dragons. When you are ready to end the meditation, thank the dragons for their help. Follow the dim corridor upward until you reach the cave opening. Think of your physical body and you will return at once.

When you are once more in your physical body, take several deep breaths to ground yourself. Open your eyes. You are once more entirely in the physical realm.

Bibliography

Campbell, Joseph. *Masks of God, Vol. 2 & 3*. New York: Penguin Books, 1976.

———. *The Power of Myth*. New York: Doubleday, 1988.

Cavendish, Richard, ed. *Mythology: An Illustrated Encyclopedia*. New York: Rizzoli, 1980.

Cirlot, J. E. *A Dictionary of Symbols*. New York: Philosophical Library, 1978.

Conway, D. J. *Dancing With Dragons*. St. Paul, MN: Llewellyn Publications, 1994.

Dennys, Rodney. *The Heraldic Imagination*. New York: Clarkson N. Potter, 1975.

Dickinson, Peter. *The Flight of Dragons*. New York: Harper & Row, 1979.

Fox-Davies, A. C. *A Complete Guide to Heraldry*. New York: Bonanza Books, 1978.

Grimal, Pierre, ed. *Larousse Encyclopedia of Mythology*. New York: Hamlyn, 1978.

Hall, Manly P. *The Secret Teachings of All Ages*. Los Angeles, CA: Philosophical Research Society, 1977.

Hogarth, Peter. *Dragons*. New York: Viking Press, 1979.

Hoult, Janet. *Dragons: Their History & Symbolism*. UK: Gothic Image, 1990.

Huxley, Francis. *The Dragon: Nature of Spirit, Spirit of Nature*. UK: Thames & Hudson, 1979.

Jung, Carl G. trans. R. F. C. Hull. *The Archetypes & the Collective Unconscious*. Princeton, NJ: Princeton University Press, 1990.

MacKenzie, Donald G. *German Myths & Legends*. New York: Avenel, 1985.

Sjoo, Monica & Barbara Mor. *The Great Cosmic Mother: Rediscovering the Religion of the Earth*. San Francisco, CA: Harper & Row, 1987.

Walker, Barbara. *The Woman's Dictionary of Symbols & Sacred Objects*. San Francisco, CA: Harper & Row, 1988.

Appendix A

Candle Colors and Uses

Black: Reversing; uncrossing; binding negative forces; resolving discord; protection; releasing; to strengthen will power; repelling dark magick and negative thoughtforms.

- Attracts dragons of Earth and Chaos, and Guardian dragons.

Blue: Truth; inspiration; wisdom; occult power; protection; understanding; good health; happiness; peace; fidelity; harmony in the home; patience.

- Attracts dragons of Water, Lakes, Seas, the Moon, Wind, and Storm (dark candles), and Guardian dragons.

Brown: To attract money and financial success; to influence Earth Elementals; concentration; balance; ESP; intuition; study.

- Attracts dragons of Earth, Mountains, and Forest, and Guardian dragons.

Gold or Very Clear Yellow: Great fortune; intuition; understanding; divination; fast luck; financial benefits; to attract higher influences.

- Attracts dragons of the Sun and Guardian dragons.

Gray: To keep someone from seeing your real actions; to hide something behind an illusion.

- Attracts dragons of Chaos and Light.

Green: Abundance; fertility; good fortune; generosity; money; wealth; success; renewal; marriage; balance.

- Attracts dragons of Earth, Forest, and Mountains and Guardian dragons.

Indigo: Meditation; to neutralize another's magick; to stop gossip, lies, or undesirable competition; to balance out karma.

- Attracts dragons of Chaos, Light, and Seas and Guardian dragons.

Magenta: Very high vibrational frequency that tends to cause the color magick of other candles to work fast, so it is usually burned with other candles; quick changes; spiritual healing; exorcism.

- Attracts dragons of Chaos (darker candles) and Light (lighter candles).

Orange: Encouragement; adaptability; stimulation; attraction; sudden changes; control; power; to draw good things; to change luck.

- Attracts dragons of Fire and Guardian dragons.

Pink: Love; affection; romance; spiritual awakening; healing of the spirit; togetherness.

- Attracts dragons of Water.

Purple or Violet: Success; idealism; higher psychic ability; wisdom; progress; protection; honors; spirit contact; to break bad luck; to drive away evil; divination.

- Attracts dragons of Water, the Moon (lavender candles), and Chaos (darker candles).

Red: Physical power; health; energy; strength; sexual potency; courage; willpower; to conquer fear or laziness.

- Attracts dragons of Fire and Guardian dragons.

Silver or Very Clear Light Gray: To remove negative powers; victory; stability; meditation; to develop psychic abilities.

- Attracts dragons of Chaos (pewter candles) and the Moon, and Guardian dragons.

White: Purity; spirituality and greater attainments in life; truth; sincerity; power of a higher nature; wholeness.

- Attracts dragons of Light, Spirit, and the Moon, and Guardian dragons.

Yellow: Intellect; imagination; power of the mind; creativity; confidence; gentle persuasion; action; attraction; concentration; inspiration; sudden changes.

- Attracts dragons of Air, the Sun, Fire, Wind, and Storm (darker candles), and Guardian dragons.

Appendix B

Stone Powers

Pyrite, also known as Fool's Gold, attracts dragons. It can be used alone or with other stones in spells for money, prosperity, and success.

Moonstone is very attractive to dragons. It can be used in spell-workings for gaining occult and/or psychic powers, divination, and a gentle, steady protection.

Clear Quartz Crystal has long been known to amplify magickal power and psychic work. Earth dragons are particularly drawn to this stone, but it attracts all dragons. This stone can be used in any spell.

Lodestone or Magnets are representative of stars and meteorites, which have always been associated with dragons. Use this stone in any spell of attracting.

Eye Stones are represented by Hawk's Eye, Cat's Eye, Tiger's Eye, etc. The pupil in a dragon's eye resembles a cat's eye with its vertical slit. The shimmer across eye stones is very similar to that seen in dragon eyes. Use these stones in spells for increasing wealth, protection, insight into problems, healing, luck, and courage.

Geodes are useful when meditating on dragons and the cave of initiation.

Staurolite is a natural stone formation that looks like an X; it is also called faery cross. It is symbolic of the four Elements with which the magician works.

Meteorite or Tektite is rock that falls from space. It is especially good for traveling from one plane of existence to another; in other words, astral travel during meditation.

Index

Dancing with Dragons

Invoke Their Ageless
Wisdom & Power

D. J. Conway

You can access one of the most potent life forces in the astral universe: the wise and magickal dragon. Dragons do exist! They inhabit the astral plane that interpenetrates our physical world. Now, *Dancing with Dragons* makes a vast and wonderful hoard of dragon magick and power available to you.

Dancing with Dragons is a ritual textbook that will teach you to call, befriend, and utilize the wisdom of these powerful mythical creatures for increased spiritual fulfillment, knowledge, health, and happiness. Here you will find complete, practical information for working with dragons: spells and rituals ranging from simple to advanced workings; designing ritual tools to aid you in using dragon energy; channeling power using the lines of dragon's breath (energy lines that run through the Earth); and using the true language of dragons in ritual and spell-casting with herbs, oils, stones, and candles.

Dancing with Dragons is a joyful experience. Whether you are a practicing magician, a devotee of role-playing games, or a seeker who wishes to tap the dragon's vast astral power, this book will help you forge a friendship and magickal partnership with these astral creatures.

1–56718–165–1, 320 pp., 7 x 10, illus., softcover $14.95

The Shapeshifter Tarot

D. J. Conway and Sirona Knight
Illustrated by Lisa Hunt

Like the ancient Celts, you can now practice the shamanic art of shapeshifting and access the knowledge of the eagle, the oak tree or the ocean: wisdom that is inherently yours and resides within your very being. The Shapeshifter Tarot kit is your bridge between humans, animals and nature. The cards in this deck act as merging tools, allowing you to tap into the many different animal energies, together with the elemental qualities of air, fire, water and earth.

The accompanying book gives detailed explanations on how to use the cards, along with their full esoteric meanings, and mythological and magical roots. Exercises in shapeshifting, moving through gateways, doubling out, meditation and guided imagery give you the opportunity to enhance your levels of perception and awareness, allowing you to hone and accentuate your magical understanding and skill.

1–56718–384–0, boxed kit:

81 cards, 260 pp., 6 x 9, illus., softcover book $29.95

The Sacred Circle Tarot

A Celtic Pagan Journey

Anna Franklin

Illustrated by Paul Mason

The Sacred Circle Tarot is a new concept in tarot design, combining photographs, computer imaging and traditional drawing techniques to create stunning images. It draws on the Pagan heritage of Britain and Ireland, its sacred sites and landscapes. Key symbols unlock the deepest levels of Pagan teaching.

The imagery of the cards is designed to work on a number of levels, serving as a tool not only for divination but to facilitate meditation, personal growth and spiritual development. The "sacred circle" refers to the progress of the initiate from undirected energy, through dawning consciousness, to the death of the old self and the emergence of the new.

The major arcana is modified somewhat to fit the pagan theme of the deck. For example, "The Fool" becomes "The Green Man," "The Heirophant" becomes "The Druid," and "The World" becomes "The World Tree." The accompanying book gives a full explanation of the symbolism in the cards and their divinatory meanings.

1–56718–457–X, boxed kit:

78 full-color cards; 288 pp., 6 x 9, illus., book $29.95

Celtic Magic

D. J. Conway

Many people, not all of Irish descent, have a great interest in the ancient Celts and the Celtic pantheon, and *Celtic Magic* is the map they need for exploring this ancient and fascinating magical culture.

Celtic Magic is for the reader who is either a beginner or intermediate in the field of magic. It provides an extensive "how-to" of practical spell-working. There are many books on the market dealing with the Celts and their beliefs, but none guide the reader to a practical application of magical knowledge for use in everyday life. There is also an in-depth discussion of Celtic deities and the Celtic way of life and worship, so that an intermediate practitioner can expand upon the spellwork to build a series of magical rituals. Presented in an easy-to-understand format, *Celtic Magic* is for anyone searching for new spells that can be worked immediately, without elaborate or rare materials, and with minimal time and preparation.

0–87542–136–9, 240 pp., mass market, illus. $4.99

Legend

The Arthurian Tarot

Anna-Marie Ferguson

Gallery artist and writer Anna—Marie Ferguson has paired the ancient divinatory system of the tarot with the Arthurian myth to create *Legend: The Arthurian Tarot*. The exquisitely beautiful watercolor paintings of this tarot deck illustrate characters, places and tales from the legends that blend traditional tarot symbolism with the Pagan and Christian symbolism that are equally significant elements of this myth.

Each card represents the Arthurian counterpart to tarot's traditional figures, such as Merlin as the Magician, Morgan le Fay as the Moon, Mordred as the King of Swords and Arthur as the Emperor. Accompanying the deck is a decorative layout sheet in the format of the Celtic Cross to inspire and guide your readings, as well as the book *Keeper of Words*, which lists the divinatory meanings of the cards, the cards' symbolism and the telling of the legend associated with each card.

This visionary tarot encompasses all the complex situations life has to offer—trials, challenge, and rewards—to help you cultivate a close awareness of your past, present and future through the richness of the Arthurian legend.

1–56718–267–4, boxed set:

78 full-color cards, 272 pp., 6 x 9, illus., softcover book, and 21" x 24" layout sheet $34.95